BLAKE

....

POEMS

EVERYMAN'S LIBRARY
POCKET POETS

Alfred A. Knopf New York London Toronto

THIS IS A BORZOI BOOK
PUBLISHED BY ALFRED A. KNOPF

This selection by Peter Washington first published in
Everyman's Library, 1994
Copyright © 1994 by Everyman's Library

Tenth printing (US)

US website: www.randomhouse.com/everymans

ISBN 0-679-43633-2 (US)
1-85715-710-9 (UK)

A CIP catalogue record for this book is available from the British Library

Typography by Peter B. Willberg
Typeset in the UK by AccComputing, North Barrow, Somerset
Printed and bound in Germany by GGP Media GmbH, Pössneck

CONTENTS

6

POEMS FROM BLAKE'S MS. BOOK

WILLIAM
BLAKE

·················

POEMS

To The Accuser who is
The God of This World

Truly, My Satan, thou art but a Dunce,
And dost not know the Garment from the Man.
Every Harlot was a Virgin once,
Nor canst thou ever change Kate into Nan.

Tho' thou art Worship'd by the Names Divine
Of Jesus & Jehovah, thou art still
The Son of Morn in weary Night's decline,
The lost Traveller's Dream under the Hill.

SONGS OF
INNOCENCE
AND OF
EXPERIENCE

*Shewing the Two Contrary States
of the Human Soul*

SONGS OF INNOCENCE
INTRODUCTION

Piping down the valleys wild,
Piping songs of pleasant glee,
On a cloud I saw a child,
And he laughing said to me:

'Pipe a song about a Lamb!'
So I piped with merry chear.
'Piper, pipe that song again;'
So I piped: he wept to hear.

'Drop thy pipe, thy happy pipe,
Sing thy songs of happy chear.'
So I sung the same again
While he wept with joy to hear.

'Piper, sit thee down and write
In a book that all may read.'
So he vanish'd from my sight,
And I pluck'd a hollow reed,

And I made a rural pen,
And I stain'd the water clear,
And I wrote my happy songs
Every child may joy to hear.

THE SHEPHERD

How sweet is the Shepherd's sweet lot!
From the morn to the evening he strays;
He shall follow his sheep all the day,
And his tongue shall be filled with praise.

For he hears the lambs' innocent call,
And he hears the ewes' tender reply;
He is watchful, while they are in peace
For they know when their Shepherd is nigh.

THE ECCHOING GREEN

The Sun does arise
And make happy the skies,
The merry bells ring
To welcome the Spring,
The sky-lark and thrush,
The birds of the bush,
Sing louder around
To the bells' chearful sound,
While our sports shall be seen
On the Ecchoing Green.

Old John with white hair
Does laugh away care,
Sitting under the oak
Among the old folk.
They laugh at our play,
And soon they all say:
'Such, such were the joys
When we all, girls & boys,
In our youth-time were seen
On the Ecchoing Green.'

Till the little ones, weary,
No more can be merry;
The sun does descend,
And our sports have an end.
Round the laps of their mothers
Many sisters and brothers,
Like birds in their nest,
Are ready for rest,
And sport no more seen
On the darkening Green.

THE LAMB

Little Lamb, who made thee:
  Dost thou know who made thee?
Gave thee life & bid thee feed
By the stream & o'er the mead;
Gave thee clothing of delight,
Softest clothing, wooly, bright;
Gave thee such a tender voice
Making all the vales rejoice?
  Little Lamb, who made thee?
  Dost thou know who made thee?

Little Lamb, I'll tell thee,
  Little Lamb, I'll tell thee:
He is called by thy name,
For he calls himself a Lamb.
He is meek & he is mild;
He became a little child:
I a child & thou a lamb,
We are called by his name.
  Little Lamb, God bless thee.
  Little Lamb, God bless thee.

THE LITTLE BLACK BOY

My mother bore me in the southern wild,
And I am black, but O! my soul is white;
White as an angel is the English child,
But I am black, as if bereav'd of light.

My mother taught me underneath a tree,
And sitting down before the heat of day
She took me on her lap and kissed me,
And pointing to the east, began to say:

'Look on the rising sun! there God does live,
And gives his light and gives his heat away;
And flowers and trees and beasts and men recieve
Comfort in morning, joy in the noon day.

'And we are put on earth a little space
That we may learn to bear the beams of love;
And these black bodies and this sun-burnt face
Is but a cloud, and like a shady grove;

'For when our souls have learn'd the heat to bear,
The cloud will vanish: we shall hear his voice,
Saying: "come out from the grove, my love & care,
And round my golden tent like lambs rejoice." '

Thus did my mother say, and kissed me.
And thus I say to little English boy:
When I from black and he from white cloud free
And round the tent of God like lambs we joy,

I'll shade him from the heat, till he can bear
To lean in joy upon our father's knee;
And then I'll stand and stroke his silver hair,
And be like him, and he will then love me.

THE BLOSSOM

Merry Merry Sparrow,
Under leaves so green,
A happy Blossom
Sees you swift as arrow
Seek your cradle narrow
Near my Bosom.

Pretty Pretty Robin,
Under leaves so green,
A happy Blossom
Hears you sobbing, sobbing.
Pretty Pretty Robin
Near my Bosom.

THE CHIMNEY SWEEPER

When my mother died I was very young,
And my father sold me while yet my tongue
Could scarcely cry 'weep, weep, weep, weep,'
So your chimneys I sweep & in soot I sleep.

There's little Tom Dacre who cried when his head,
That curl'd like a lamb's back, was shav'd: so I said,
'Hush, Tom, never mind it, for when your head's bare
You know that the soot cannot spoil your white hair.'

And so he was quiet, & that very night,
As Tom was a sleeping, he had such a sight,
That thousands of sweepers, Dick, Joe, Ned & Jack,
Were all of them lock'd up in coffins of black.

And by came an Angel who had a bright key,
And he open'd the coffins & set them all free;
Then down a green plain, leaping, laughing, they run,
And wash in a river, and shine in the Sun.

Then naked & white, all their bags left behind,
They rise upon clouds, and sport in the wind;
And the Angel told Tom, if he'd be a good boy,
He'd have God for his father & never want joy.

And so Tom awoke; and we rose in the dark,
And got with our bags & our brushes to work.
Tho' the morning was cold, Tom was happy & warm;
So if all do their duty they need not fear harm.

THE LITTLE BOY LOST

'Father, father, where are you going?
O do not walk so fast.
Speak father, speak to your little boy,
Or else I shall be lost.'

The night was dark, no father was there;
The child was wet with dew;
The mire was deep, & the child did weep,
And away the vapour flew.

THE LITTLE BOY FOUND

The little boy lost in the lonely fen,
Led by the wand'ring light,
Began to cry, but God ever nigh,
Appear'd like his father in white.

He kissed the child & by the hand led
And to his mother brought,
Who in sorrow pale, thro' the lonely dale,
Her little boy weeping sought.

LAUGHING SONG

When the green woods laugh with the voice of joy,
And the dimpling stream runs laughing by,
When the air does laugh with our merry wit,
And the green hill laughs with the noise of it,

When the meadows laugh with lively green,
And the grasshopper laughs in the merry scene,
When Mary and Susan and Emily
With their sweet round mouths sing 'Ha, Ha, He!'

When the painted birds laugh in the shade
Where our table with cherries and nuts is spread,
Come live & be merry and join with me,
To sing the sweet chorus of 'Ha, Ha, He!'

A CRADLE SONG

Sweet dreams, form a shade
O'er my lovely infant's head,
Sweet dreams of pleasant streams
By happy silent moony beams.

Sweet sleep, with soft down
Weave thy brows an infant crown.
Sweet sleep, Angel mild,
Hover o'er my happy child.

Sweet smiles, in the night
Hover over my delight;
Sweet smiles, Mother's smiles,
All the livelong night beguiles.

Sweet moans, dovelike sighs
Chase not slumber from thy eyes.
Sweet moans, sweeter smiles
All the dovelike moans beguiles.

Sleep, sleep, happy child,
All creation slept and smil'd;
Sleep, sleep, happy sleep,
While o'er thee thy mother weep.

Sweet babe, in thy face
Holy image I can trace.
Sweet babe, once like thee
Thy maker lay and wept for me:

Wept for me, for thee, for all,
When he was an infant small.
Thou his image ever see,
Heavenly face that smiles on thee:

Smiles on thee, on me, on all,
Who became an infant small.
Infant smiles are his own smiles,
Heaven & earth to peace beguiles.

THE DIVINE IMAGE

To Mercy Pity Peace and Love
All pray in their distress,
And to these virtues of delight
Return their thankfulness.

For Mercy Pity Peace and Love
Is God our father dear,
And Mercy Pity Peace and Love
Is Man his child and care.

For Mercy has a human heart,
Pity, a human face,
And Love, the human form divine,
And Peace, the human dress.

Then every man of every clime
That prays in his distress,
Prays to the human form divine,
Love Mercy Pity Peace.

And all must love the human form
In heathen, turk or jew.
Where Mercy Love & Pity dwell
There God is dwelling too.

HOLY THURSDAY

'Twas on a Holy Thursday, their innocent faces clean,
The children walking two & two, in red & blue &
    green,
Grey headed beadles walk'd before, with wands as
    white as snow,
Till into the high dome of Paul's they like Thames'
    waters flow.

O what a multitude they seem'd, these flowers of
    London town!
Seated in companies they sit with radiance all their
    own.
The hum of multitudes was there, but multitudes of
    lambs,
Thousands of little boys & girls raising their innocent
    hands.

Now like a mighty wind they raise to heaven the voice
    of song,
Or like harmonious thunderings the seats of heaven
    among.
Beneath them sit the aged men, wise guardians of the
    poor;
Then cherish pity, lest you drive an angel from your
    door.

NIGHT

The sun descending in the west
The evening star does shine,
The birds are silent in their nest
And I must seek for mine,
The moon, like a flower
In heaven's high bower,
With silent delight
Sits and smiles on the night.

Farewell green fields and happy groves
Where flocks have took delight;
Where lambs have nibbled, silent moves
The feet of angels bright;
Unseen they pour blessing
And joy without ceasing
On each bud and blossom
And each sleeping bosom.

They look in every thoughtless nest
Where birds are cover'd warm,
They visit caves of every beast
To keep them all from harm;
If they see any weeping
That should have been sleeping,
They pour sleep on their head
And sit down by their bed.

When wolves and tygers howl for prey
They pitying stand and weep,
Seeking to drive their thirst away
And keep them from the sheep;
But if they rush dreadful,
The angels most heedful
Recieve each mild spirit
New worlds to inherit.

And there the lion's ruddy eyes
Shall flow with tears of gold,
And pitying the tender cries
And walking round the fold
Saying, 'wrath, by his meekness,
And by his health, sickness
Is driven away
From our immortal day.

'And now beside thee, bleating lamb,
I can lie down and sleep,
Or think on him who bore thy name,
Graze after thee and weep;
For, wash'd in life's river,
My bright mane for ever
Shall shine like the gold
As I guard o'er the fold.'

SPRING

Sound the Flute!
Now it's mute.
Birds delight
Day and Night;
Nightingale
In the dale,
Lark in Sky,
Merrily,
Merrily, Merrily, to welcome in the Year.

Little Boy
Full of joy,
Little Girl
Sweet and small,
Cock does crow,
So do you;
Merry voice,
Infant noise,
Merrily, Merrily, to welcome in the Year.

Little Lamb
Here I am,
Come and lick
My white neck,
Let me pull
Your soft Wool,
Let me kiss
Your soft face;
Merrily, Merrily we welcome in the Year.

NURSE'S SONG

When the voices of children are heard on the green
And laughing is heard on the hill,
My heart is at rest within my breast
And every thing else is still.

'Then come home, my children, the sun is gone down
And the dews of night arise;
Come, come, leave off play, and let us away
Till the morning appears in the skies.'

'No, no, let us play, for it is yet day
And we cannot go to sleep;
Besides, in the sky the little birds fly
And the hills are all cover'd with sheep.'

'Well, well, go & play till the light fades away
And then go home to bed.'
The little ones leaped & shouted & laugh'd
And all the hills ecchoed.

INFANT JOY

'I have no name:
I am but two days old.'
What shall I call thee?
'I happy am,
Joy is my name.'
Sweet joy befall thee!

Pretty joy!
Sweet joy but two days old,
Sweet joy I call thee:
Thou dost smile,
I sing the while
Sweet joy befall thee.

A DREAM

Once a dream did weave a shade
O'er my Angel-guarded bed,
That an Emmet lost its way
Where on grass methought I lay.

Troubled, 'wilder'd and folorn,
Dark, benighted, travel-worn,
Over many a tangled spray,
All heart-broke I heard her say:

'O my children! do they cry?
Do they hear their father sigh?
Now they look abroad to see,
Now return and weep for me.'

Pitying, I dropp'd a tear;
But I saw a glow-worm near,
Who replied: 'What wailing wight
Calls the watchman of the night?

'I am set to light the ground,
While the beetle goes his round:
Follow now the beetle's hum;
Little wanderer, hie thee home.'

ON ANOTHER'S SORROW

Can I see another's woe
And not be in sorrow too?
Can I see another's grief
And not seek for kind relief?

Can I see a falling tear
And not feel my sorrow's share?
Can a father see his child
Weep, nor be with sorrow fill'd?

Can a mother sit and hear
An infant groan an infant fear?
No, no never can it be,
Never, never can it be.

And can he who smiles on all
Hear the wren with sorrows small,
Hear the small bird's grief & care,
Hear the woes that infants bear,

And not sit beside the nest
Pouring pity in their breast,
And not sit the cradle near
Weeping tear on infant's tear,

And not sit both night & day
Wiping all our tears away?
O! no never can it be,
Never, never can it be.

He doth give his joy to all,
He becomes an infant small,
He becomes a man of woe,
He doth feel the sorrow too.

Think not thou canst sigh a sigh
And thy maker is not by;
Think not thou canst weep a tear
And thy maker is not near.

O! he gives to us his joy
That our grief he may destroy;
Till our grief is fled & gone
He doth sit by us and moan.

SONGS OF EXPERIENCE
INTRODUCTION

Hear the voice of the Bard!
Who Present, Past, & Future sees,
Whose ears have heard
The Holy Word
That walk'd among the ancient trees,

Calling the lapsed Soul,
And weeping in the evening dew,
That might controll
The starry pole
And fallen fallen light renew!

'O Earth, O Earth return!
Arise from out the dewy grass;
Night is worn
And the morn
Rises from the slumberous mass.

'Turn away no more:
Why wilt thou turn away?
The starry floor
The wat'ry shore
Is giv'n thee till the break of day.'

EARTH'S ANSWER

Earth rais'd up her head
From the darkness dread & drear.
Her light fled:
Stony dread!
And her locks cover'd with grey despair.

'Prison'd on wat'ry shore,
Starry Jealousy does keep my den
Cold and hoar;
Weeping o'er,
I hear the father of the ancient men.

'Selfish father of men,
Cruel jealous, selfish fear:
Can delight,
Chain'd in night,
The virgins of youth and morning bear?

'Does spring hide its joy
When buds and blossoms grow?
Does the sower
Sow by night?
Or the plowman in darkness plow?

'Break this heavy chain
That does freeze my bones around.
Selfish! vain!
Eternal bane!
That free Love with bondage bound.'

THE CLOD & THE PEBBLE

'Love seeketh not Itself to please
Nor for itself hath any care,
But for another gives its ease
And builds a Heaven in Hell's despair.'

So sung a little Clod of Clay
Trodden with the cattle's feet,
But a Pebble of the brook
Warbled out these metres meet:

'Love seeketh only Self to please,
To bind another to Its delight,
Joys in another's loss of ease,
And builds a Hell in Heaven's despite.'

HOLY THURSDAY

Is this a holy thing to see
In a rich and fruitful land,
Babes reduc'd to misery,
Fed with cold and usurous hand?

Is that trembling cry a song?
Can it be a song of joy?
And so many children poor?
It is a land of poverty!

And their sun does never shine,
And their fields are bleak & bare,
And their ways are fill'd with thorns:
It is eternal winter there.

For where-e'er the sun does shine,
And where-e'er the rain does fall,
Babe can never hunger there,
Nor poverty the mind appall.

THE LITTLE GIRL LOST

In futurity
I prophetic see
That the earth from sleep
(Grave the sentence deep)

Shall arise and seek
For her maker meek,
And the desart wild
Become a garden mild.

In the southern clime
Where the summer's prime
Never fades away,
Lovely Lyca lay.

Seven summers old
Lovely Lyca told;
She had wander'd long
Hearing wild birds' song.

'Sweet sleep, come to me
Underneath this tree.
Do father, mother, weep,
Where can Lyca sleep?

'Lost in desart wild
Is your little child.
How can Lyca sleep
If her mother weep?

'If her heart does ake
Then let Lyca wake;
If my mother sleep,
Lyca shall not weep.

'Frowning frowning night,
O'er this desart bright
Let thy moon arise
While I close my eyes.'

Sleeping Lyca lay
While the beasts of prey,
Come from caverns deep,
View'd the maid asleep.

The kingly lion stood
And the virgin view'd,
Then he gambol'd round
O'er the hallow'd ground.

Leopards, tygers play
Round her as she lay,
While the lion old
Bow'd his mane of gold,

And her bosom lick,
And upon her neck
From his eyes of flame
Ruby tears there came;

While the lioness
Loos'd her slender dress,
And naked they convey'd
To caves the sleeping maid.

THE LITTLE GIRL FOUND

All the night in woe
Lyca's parents go
Over vallies deep,
While the desarts weep.

Tired and woe-begone,
Hoarse with making moan,
Arm in arm seven days
They trac'd the desart ways.

Seven nights they sleep
Among shadows deep,
And dream they see their child
Starv'd in desart wild.

Pale, thro' pathless ways
The fancied image strays,
Famish'd, weeping, weak
With hollow piteous shriek.

Rising from unrest,
The trembling woman prest
With feet of weary woe:
She could no further go.

In his arms he bore
Her arm'd with sorrow sore,
Till before their way
A couching lion lay.

Turning back was vain:
Soon his heavy mane
Bore them to the ground,
Then he stalk'd around

Smelling to his prey,
But their fears allay
When he licks their hands
And silent by them stands.

They look upon his eyes
Fill'd with deep surprise,
And wondering behold
A spirit arm'd in gold.

On his head a crown,
On his shoulders down
Flow'd his golden hair.
Gone was all their care.

'Follow me,' he said;
'Weep not for the maid;
In my palace deep
Lyca lies asleep.'

Then they followed
Where the vision led,
And saw their sleeping child
Among tygers wild.

To this day they dwell
In a lonely dell,
Nor fear the wolvish howl
Nor the lion's growl.

THE CHIMNEY SWEEPER

A little black thing among the snow,
Crying 'weep, weep,' in notes of woe!
'Where are thy father & mother, say?'
'They are both gone up to the church to pray.

'Because I was happy upon the heath,
And smil'd among the winter's snow,
They clothed me in the clothes of death,
And taught me to sing the notes of woe.

'And because I am happy, & dance & sing,
They think they have done me no injury,
And are gone to praise God & his Priest & King,
Who make up a heaven of our misery.'

NURSE'S SONG

When the voices of children are heard on the green
And whisp'rings are in the dale,
The days of my youth rise fresh in my mind:
My face turns green and pale.

Then come home my children, the sun is gone down
And the dews of night arise;
Your spring & your day are wasted in play,
And your winter and night in disguise.

THE SICK ROSE

O rose, thou art sick:
The invisible worm
That flies in the night
In the howling storm,

Has found out thy bed
Of crimson joy,
And his dark secret love
Does thy life destroy.

THE FLY

Little Fly,
Thy summer's play
My thoughtless hand
Has brush'd away.

Am not I
A fly like thee?
Or art not thou
A man like me?

For I dance
And drink & sing,
Till some blind hand
Shall brush my wing.

If thought is life
And strength & breath,
And the want
Of thought is death,

Then am I
A happy fly
If I live
Or if I die.

THE ANGEL

I Dreamt a Dream! what can it mean?
And that I was a maiden Queen
Guarded by an Angel mild:
Witless woe was ne'er beguil'd!

And I wept both night and day,
And he wip'd my tears away,
And I wept both day and night,
And hid from him my heart's delight.

So he took his wings and fled;
Then the morn blush'd rosy red;
I dried my tears & arm'd my fears
With ten thousand shields and spears.

Soon my Angel came again:
I was arm'd, he came in vain,
For the time of youth was fled
And grey hairs were on my head.

THE TYGER

Tyger, Tyger, burning bright
In the forests of the night,
What immortal hand or eye
Could frame thy fearful symmetry?

In what distant deeps or skies
Burnt the fire of thine eyes?
On what wings dare he aspire?
What the hand dare sieze the fire?

And what shoulder, & what art,
Could twist the sinews of thy heart?
And when thy heart began to beat,
What dread hand? & what dread feet?

What the hammer? what the chain,
In what furnace was thy brain?
What the anvil? what dread grasp
Dare its deadly terrors clasp?

When the stars threw down their spears
And water'd heaven with their tears,
Did he smile his work to see?
Did he who made the Lamb make thee?

Tyger, Tyger, burning bright
In the forests of the night,
What immortal hand or eye
Dare frame thy fearful symmetry?

MY PRETTY ROSE TREE

A flower was offer'd to me,
Such a flower as May never bore;
But I said 'I've a Pretty Rose-tree,'
And I passed the sweet flower o'er.

Then I went to my Pretty Rose-tree,
To tend her by day and by night;
But my Rose turn'd away with jealousy,
And her thorns were my only delight.

AH! SUN-FLOWER

Ah Sun-flower! weary of time,
Who countest the steps of the Sun,
Seeking after that sweet golden clime
Where the traveller's journey is done:

Where the Youth pined away with desire,
And the pale Virgin shrouded in snow,
Arise from their graves and aspire
Where my Sun-flower wishes to go.

THE LILLY

The modest Rose puts forth a thorn,
The humble Sheep a threat'ning horn,
While the Lilly white shall in Love delight,
Nor a thorn nor a threat stain her beauty bright.

THE GARDEN OF LOVE

I went to the Garden of Love,
And saw what I never had seen:
A Chapel was built in the midst,
Where I used to play on the green.

And the gates of this Chapel were shut,
And 'Thou shalt not' writ over the door;
So I turn'd to the Garden of Love
That so many sweet flowers bore;

And I saw it was filled with graves,
And tomb-stones where flowers should be;
And Priests in black gowns were walking their
     rounds,
And binding with briars my joys & desires.

THE LITTLE VAGABOND

Dear Mother, dear Mother, the Church is cold,
But the Ale-house is healthy & pleasant & warm;
Besides I can tell where I am used well,
Such usage in heaven will never do well.

But if at the Church they would give us some Ale
And a pleasant fire our souls to regale,
We'd sing and we'd pray all the live-long day,
Nor ever once wish from the Church to stray.

Then the Parson might preach & drink & sing,
And we'd be as happy as birds in the spring;
And modest dame Lurch, who is always at Church,
Would not have bandy children, nor fasting, nor birch.

And God, like a father rejoicing to see
His children as pleasant and happy as he,
Would have no more quarrel with the Devil or the
      Barrel,
But kiss him & give him both drink and apparel.

LONDON

I wander thro' each charter'd street
Near where the charter'd Thames does flow,
And mark in every face I meet
Marks of weakness, marks of woe.

In every cry of every Man,
In every Infant's cry of fear,
In every voice, in every ban,
The mind-forg'd manacles I hear.

How the Chimney-sweeper's cry
Every black'ning Church appalls,
And the hapless Soldier's sigh
Runs in blood down Palace walls.

But most thro' midnight streets I hear
How the youthful Harlot's curse
Blasts the new born Infant's tear,
And blights with plagues the Marriage hearse.

THE HUMAN ABSTRACT

Pity would be no more
If we did not make somebody Poor;
And Mercy no more could be
If all were as happy as we.

And mutual fear brings peace,
Till the selfish loves increase:
Then Cruelty knits a snare
And spreads his baits with care

He sits down with holy fears
And waters the ground with tears:
Then Humility takes its root
Underneath his foot.

Soon spreads the dismal shade
Of Mystery over his head,
And the Catterpiller and Fly
Feed on the Mystery.

And it bears the fruit of Deceit,
Ruddy and sweet to eat,
And the Raven his nest has made
In its thickest shade.

The Gods of the earth and sea
Sought thro' Nature to find this Tree,
But their search was all in vain:
There grows one in the Human Brain.

INFANT SORROW

My mother groan'd! my father wept,
Into the dangerous world I leapt,
Helpless, naked, piping loud,
Like a fiend hid in a cloud.

Struggling in my father's hands,
Striving against my swadling bands,
Bound and weary, I thought best
To sulk upon my mother's breast.

A POISON TREE

I was angry with my friend,
I told my wrath, my wrath did end;
I was angry with my foe,
I told it not, my wrath did grow.

And I water'd it in fears,
Night & morning with my tears;
And I sunned it with smiles,
And with soft deceitful wiles.

And it grew both day and night,
Till it bore an apple bright;
And my foe beheld it shine,
And he knew that it was mine,

And into my garden stole
When the night had veil'd the pole:
In the morning glad I see
My foe outstretch'd beneath the tree.

LITTLE BOY LOST

'Nought loves another as itself,
Nor venerates another so,
Nor is it possible to Thought
A greater than itself to know:

'And Father, how can I love you
Or any of my brothers more?
I love you like the little bird
That picks up crumbs around the door.'

The Priest sat by and heard the child,
In trembling zeal he siez'd his hair:
He led him by his little coat,
And all admir'd the Priestly care.

And standing on the altar high,
'Lo, what a fiend is here!' said he,
'One who sets reason up for judge
Of our most holy Mystery.'

The weeping child could not be heard,
The weeping parents wept in vain;
They strip'd him to his little shirt,
And bound him in an iron chain;

And burn'd him in a holy place,
Where many had been burn'd before:
The weeping parents wept in vain.
Are such things done on Albion's shore?

A LITTLE GIRL LOST

Children of the future Age
Reading this indignant page,
Know that in a former time
Love! sweet Love! was thought a crime.

In the Age of Gold,
Free from winter's cold,
Youth and maiden bright
To the holy light,
Naked in the sunny beams delight.

Once a youthful pair,
Fill'd with softest care,
Met in garden bright
Where the holy light
Had just remov'd the curtains of the night.

There, in rising day,
On the grass they play;
Parents were afar,
Strangers came not near,
And the maiden soon forgot her fear.

Tired with kisses sweet,
They agree to meet
When the silent sleep
Waves o'er heaven's deep,
And the weary tired wanderers weep.

To her father white
Came the maiden bright;
But his loving look,
Like the holy book,
All her tender limbs with terror shook.

'Ona! pale and weak!
To thy father speak:
O the trembling fear!
O the dismal care!
That shakes the blossoms of my hoary hair.'

TO TIRZAH

Whate'er is Born of Mortal Birth
Must be consumed with the Earth
To rise from Generation free:
Then what have I to do with thee?

The Sexes sprung from Shame & Pride,
Blow'd in the morn, in evening died;
But Mercy chang'd Death into Sleep;
The Sexes rose to work & weep.

Thou Mother of my Mortal part,
With cruelty didst mould my Heart,
And with false self-decieving tears
Didst bind my Nostrils Eyes & Ears:

Didst close my Tongue in senseless clay,
And me to Mortal Life betray.
The Death of Jesus set me free:
Then what have I to do with thee?

THE SCHOOL BOY

I love to rise in a summer morn
When the birds sing on every tree;
The distant huntsman winds his horn,
And the sky-lark sings with me.
O! what sweet company.

But to go to school in a summer morn,
O! it drives all joy away;
Under a cruel eye outworn
The little ones spend the day
In sighing and dismay.

Ah! then at times I drooping sit,
And spend many an anxious hour,
Nor in my book can I take delight,
Nor sit in learning's bower,
Worn thro' with the dreary shower.

How can the bird that is born for joy
Sit in a cage and sing?
How can a child when fears annoy
But droop his tender wing
And forget his youthful spring?

O! father & mother, if buds are nip'd
And blossoms blown away,
And if the tender plants are strip'd
Of their joy in the springing day,
By sorrow and care's dismay,

How shall the summer arise in joy,
Or the summer fruits appear?
Or how shall we gather what griefs destroy,
Or bless the mellowing year
When the blasts of winter appear?

THE VOICE OF THE ANCIENT BARD

Youth of delight, come hither
And see the opening morn,
Image of truth new born.
Doubt is fled & clouds of reason,
Dark disputes & artful teazing.
Folly is an endless maze,
Tangled roots perplex her ways,
How many have fallen there!
They stumble all night over bones of the dead,
And feel they know not what but care,
And wish to lead others when they should be led.

A DIVINE IMAGE

Cruelty has a Human Heart,
And Jealousy a Human Face;
Terror the Human Form Divine,
And Secrecy the Human Dress.

The Human Dress is forged Iron,
The Human Form a fiery Forge,
The Human Face a Furnace seal'd,
The Human Heart its hungry Gorge.

NOTE – *Blake etched the above upon a copper plate in his usual manner, but as he never included the verses in any copy of the 'Songs of Experience' they may safely be regarded as having been rejected by him.*

POEMS FROM BLAKE'S MS. BOOK

(About 1793)

(When Blake was writing the 'Songs of Experience' he turned his sketch-book upside down and copied the poems neatly on to its last pages. When he came to print the 'Songs of Experience' he appears to have made a very careful selection from these poems, choosing from variants upon a theme, and rejecting when the meaning was indeterminate. We may therefore safely assume that the poems of this period which are not included in the 'Songs of Experience' were, in many cases, definitely rejected and are therefore of lesser importance than some other works existing only in manuscript – such as the Pickering MS. – which Blake might have committed to type had occasion offered. The following are the poems referred to, viz., those which remain after the drafts of the 'Songs of Experience' have been omitted.)

I told my love, I told my love,
I told her all my heart;
Trembling cold, in ghastly fears,
Ah! she doth depart.

Soon as she was gone from me
A traveller came by;
Silently, invisibly,
O! was no deny.

———

I laid me down upon a bank
Where love lay sleeping;
I heard among the rushes dank
Weeping, Weeping.

Then I went to the heath & the wild,
To the thistles & thorns of the waste,
And they told me how they were beguil'd,
Driven out & compel'd to be chaste.

I saw a chapel all of gold
That none did dare to enter in,
And many weeping stood without,
Weeping, mourning, worshipping.

I saw a serpent rise between
The white pillars of the door,
And he forc'd & forc'd & forc'd –
Down the golden hinges tore,

And along the pavement sweet,
Set with pearls & rubies bright,
All his slimy length he drew,
Till upon the altar white

Vomiting his poison out
On the bread & on the wine:
So I turn'd into a sty
And laid me down among the swine.

I asked a thief to steal me a peach,
He turned up his eyes:
I asked a lithe lady to lie her down,
Holy & meek, she cries.

As soon as I went, an angel came,
He wink'd at the thief
And smil'd at the dame,
And without one word said
Had a peach from the tree,
And still as a maid
Enjoy'd the Lady.

———

I heard an Angel singing
When the day was springing,
'Mercy, Pity, Peace
Is the world's release.'

Thus he sung all day
Over the new mown hay
Till the sun went down
And haycocks looked brown.

I heard a Devil curse
Over the heath & the furze,
'Mercy could be no more
If there was nobody poor;

'And pity no more could be
If all were as happy as we.'
At his curse the sun went down,
And the heavens gave a frown.

And Miserie's increase
Is Mercy, Pity, Peace.

A CRADLE SONG

Sleep, Sleep! beauty bright
Dreaming o'er the joys of night.
Sleep, Sleep! in thy sleep
Little sorrows sit & weep.

Sweet Babe, in thy face
Soft desires I can trace,
Secret joys & secret smiles,
Little pretty infant wiles.

As thy softest limbs I feel,
Smiles as of the morning steal
O'er thy cheek, & o'er thy breast
Where thy little heart does rest.

O! the cunning wiles that creep
In thy little heart asleep;
When thy little heart does wake
Then the dreadful lightnings break.

From thy cheek & from thy eye,
O'er the youthful harvests nigh,
Infant wiles & infant smiles
Heaven & Earth of peace beguiles.

I fear'd the fury of my wind
Would blight all blossoms fair & true,
And my sun it shin'd & shin'd,
And my wind it never blew.

But a blossom fair or true
Was not found on any tree,
For all blossoms grew & grew
Fruitless false, tho' fair to see.

———

Why should I care for the men of thames,
Or the cheating waves of charter'd streams?
Or shrink at the little blasts of fear
That the hireling blows into my ear?

Tho' born on the cheating banks of Thames,
Tho' his waters bathed my infant limbs
The Ohio shall wash his stains from me.
I was born a slave, but I go to be free.

INFANT SORROW

My mother groan'd, my father wept,
Into the dangerous world I leapt,
Helpless, naked, piping loud,
Like a fiend hid in a cloud.

Struggling in my father's hands,
Striving against my swaddling bands,
Bound & weary, I thought best
To sulk upon my mother's breast.

When I saw that rage was vain
And to sulk would nothing gain,
Turning many a trick & wile
I began to soothe & smile.

And I sooth'd day after day,
Till upon the ground I stray;
And I smil'd night after night,
Seeking only for delight.

And I saw before me shine
Clusters of the wand'ring vine,
And many a lovely flower & tree
Stretch'd their blossoms out to me.

My father then with holy look,
In his hands a holy book,
Pronounc'd curses on my head,
And bound me in a mirtle shade.

'Why should I be bound to thee
O my lovely mirtle tree?
Love, free love, cannot be bound
To any tree that grows on ground.'

O, how sick & weary I
Underneath my mirtle lie!
Like to dung upon the ground
Underneath my mirtle bound.

Oft my mirtle sigh'd in vain
To behold my heavy chain;
Oft my father saw us sigh
And laugh'd at our simplicity.

So I smote him, & his gore
Stain'd the roots my mirtle bore;
But the time of youth is fled,
And grey hairs are on my head.

Silent, Silent Night
Quench the holy light
Of thy torches bright;

For possess'd of Day
Thousand spirits stray
That sweet joys betray.

Why should joys be sweet
Used with deceit,
Nor with sorrows meet?

But an honest joy
Does itself destroy
For a harlot coy.

O lapwing, thou fliest around the heath
Nor seest the net that is spread beneath,
Why dost thou not fly among the corn fields?
They cannot spread nets where a harvest yields.

———

Thou hast a lap full of seed
And this is a fine country:
Why dost thou not cast thy seed
And live in it merrily?

Shall I cast it on the sand
And turn it into fruitful land?
For on no other ground
Can I sow my seed
Without tearing up
Some stinking weed.

THE WILD FLOWER'S SONG

As I wander'd the forest
The green leaves among,
I heard a wild flower
Singing a song:

'I slept in the Earth
In the silent night;
I murmur'd my fears
And I felt delight.

'In the morning I went
As rosy as morn
To seek for new Joy,
But O! met with scorn.'

TO NOBODADDY

Why art thou silent & invisible,
Father of Jealousy?
Why dost thou hide thyself in clouds
From every searching Eye?

Why darkness & obscurity
In all thy words & laws,
That none dare eat the fruit but from
The wily serpent's jaws?
Or is it because Secresy gains females' loud applause?

———

Are not the joys of morning sweeter
Than the joys of night?
And are the vig'rous joys of youth
Ashamed of the light?

Let age & sickness silent rob
The vineyards in the night,
But those who burn with vig'rous youth
Pluck fruits before the light.

They said this mystery never shall cease:
The priest promotes war & the soldier peace.

———

Love to faults is always blind,
Always is to joy inclin'd,
Lawless, wing'd & unconfin'd,
And breaks all chains from every mind.

———

Deceit to secresy confin'd,
Lawful, cautious & refin'd,
To every thing but interest blind,
And forges fetters for the mind.

———

There souls of men are bought & sold,
And milkfed infancy for gold,
And youth to slaughter houses led,
And beauty for a bit of bread.

SOFT SNOW

I walked abroad in a snowy day,
I ask'd the soft snow with me to play;
She play'd & she melted in all her prime,
And the winter call'd it a dreadful crime.

AN ANCIENT PROVERB

Remove away that black'ning church,
Remove away that marriage hearse,
Remove away that man of blood,
You'll quite remove the ancient curse.

MERLIN'S PROPHECY

The harvest shall flourish in wintry weather
When two virginities meet together.

The King & the Priest must be tied in a tether
Before two virgins can meet together.

DAY

The Sun arises in the East,
Cloth'd in robes of blood & gold;
Swords & spears, & wrath increast,
All around his bosom roll'd,
Crown'd with warlike fires & raging desires.

THE MARRIAGE RING

'Come hither, my sparrows,
My little arrows.
If a tear or a smile
Will a man beguile,
If an amorous delay
Clouds a sunshiny day,
If the step of a foot
Smites the heart to its root –
'Tis the marriage ring
Makes each fairy a king.'

So a fairy sung.
From the leaves I sprung.
He leap'd from the spray
To flee away,
But in my hat caught
He soon shall be taught,
Let him laugh, let him cry,
He's my butterfly,
For I've pull'd out the sting
Of the marriage ring.

ETERNITY

He who binds to himself a joy
Does the winged life destroy;
But he who kisses the joy as it flies
Lives in eternity's sun rise.

———

If you trap the moment before it's ripe,
The tears of repentance you'll certainly wipe;
But if once you let the ripe moment go
You can never wipe off the tears of woe.

The sword sung on the barren heath,
The sickle in the fruitful field;
The sword he sung a song of death,
But could not make the sickle yield.

———

Abstinence sows sand over all
The ruddy limbs & flowing hair;
But Desire Gratified
Plants fruit of life & beauty there.

———

In a wife I would desire
What in whores is always found,
The lineaments of Gratified desire.

THE QUESTION ANSWER'D

What is it men in women do require?
The lineaments of Gratified Desire.
What is it women do in men require?
The lineaments of Gratified Desire.

LACEDEMONIAN INSTRUCTION

'Come hither, my boy, tell me what thou seest there.'
'A foot tangled in a religious snare.'

RICHES

The countless gold of a merry heart,
The rubies & pearls of a loving eye,
The indolent never can bring to the mart,
Nor the secret hoard up in his treasury.

AN ANSWER TO THE PARSON

'Why of the sheep do you not learn peace?'
'Because I don't want you to shear my fleece.'

The look of love alarms
Because 'tis fill'd with fire;
But the look of soft deceit
Shall win the lover's hire.

Soft deceit & idleness,
These are beauty's sweetest dress.

———

Her whole Life is an Epigram, smart, smooth, & neatly
    pen'd,
Platted quite neat to catch applause, with a sliding
    noose at the end.

MOTTO TO THE SONGS OF INNOCENCE & OF EXPERIENCE

The Good are attracted by Men's perceptions
And think not for themselves,
Till Experience teaches them to catch
And to Cage the Fairies & Elves.

And then the Knave begins to snarl,
And the Hypocrite to howl,
And all his good Friends show their private ends,
And the Eagle is known from the Owl.

An old maid early, e'er I knew
Ought but the love that on me grew;
And now I'm cover'd o'er & o'er,
And wish that I had been a whore.

O, I cannot cannot find
The undaunted courage of a Virgin Mind;
For Early I in love was crost
Before my flower of love was lost.

————

The Angel that presided o'er my birth
Said, 'Little creature, form'd of Joy & Mirth,
Go love, without the help of any Thing on Earth.'

THE 'PICKERING' MS.

(About 1803)

THE SMILE

There is a Smile of Love,
And there is a Smile of Deceit,
And there is a Smile of Smiles
In which these two Smiles meet.

And there is a Frown of Hate,
And there is a Frown of Disdain,
And there is a Frown of Frowns
Which you strive to forget in vain;

For it sticks in the Heart's deep Core
And it sticks in the deep Back bone,
And no Smile that ever was smil'd,
But only one Smile alone,

That betwixt the Cradle & Grave
It only once Smil'd can be;
But, when it once is Smil'd,
There's an end to all Misery.

THE GOLDEN NET

Three Virgins at the break of day:
'Whither, young Man, whither away?
Alas for woe! alas for woe!'
They cry, & tears for ever flow.
The one was Cloth'd in flames of fire,
The other Cloth'd in iron wire,
The other Cloth'd in tears & sighs.
Dazling bright before my Eyes
They bore a Net of golden twine
To hang upon the Branches fine.
Pitying I wept to see the woe
That Love & Beauty undergo,
To be consum'd in burning Fires
And in ungratified Desires,
And in tears cloth'd night & day
Melted all my Soul away.
When they saw my Tears, a Smile
That did Heaven itself beguile,
Bore the Golden Net aloft
As on downy Pinions soft
. Over the Morning of my Day.
Underneath the Net I stray,
Now intreating Burning Fire,
Now intreating Iron Wire,
Now intreating Tears & Sighs,
O when will the morning rise?

THE MENTAL TRAVELLER

I travel'd thro' a Land of Men,
A Land of Men & Women too,
And heard & saw such dreadful things
As cold Earth wanderers never knew.

For there the Babe is born in joy
That was begotten in dire woe,
Just as we Reap in joy the fruit
Which we in bitter tears did sow.

And if the Babe is born a Boy
He's given to a Woman Old
Who nails him down upon a rock,
Catches his shrieks in cups of gold.

She binds iron thorns around his head,
She pierces both his hands & feet,
She cuts his heart out at his side
To make it feel both cold & heat.

Her fingers number every Nerve,
Just as a Miser counts his gold;
She lives upon his shrieks & cries,
And She grows young as he grows old.

Till he becomes a bleeding youth
And She becomes a Virgin bright;
Then he rends up his Manacles
And binds her down for his delight.

He plants himself in all her Nerves,
Just as a Husbandman his mould;
And She becomes his dwelling place
And Garden fruitful seventy fold.

An Aged Shadow, soon he fades,
Wand'ring round an Earthly Cot,
Full filled all with gems & gold
Which he by industry had got.

And these are the gems of the Human Soul,
The rubies & pearls of a lovesick eye,
The countless gold of the akeing heart,
The martyr's groan & the lover's sigh.

They are his meat, they are his drink;
He feeds the Beggar & the Poor
And the wayfaring Traveller:
For ever open is his door.

His grief is their eternal joy;
They make the roofs & walls to ring;
Till from the fire on the hearth
A little Female Babe does spring.

And She is all of solid fire
And gems & gold, that none his hand
Dares stretch to touch her Baby form,
Or wrap her in his swaddling-band.

But She comes to the Man she loves,
If young or old, or rich or poor;
They soon drive out the aged Host,
A Beggar at another's door,

He wanders weeping far away,
Untill some other take him in;
Oft blind & age-bent, sore distrest,
Untill he can a Maiden win.

And to allay his freezing Age,
The Poor Man takes her in his arms;
The Cottage fades before his sight,
The Garden & its lovely Charms.

The Guests are scatter'd thro' the land,
For the Eye altering alters all;
The Senses roll themselves in fear
And the flat Earth becomes a Ball;

The Stars, Sun, Moon, all shrink away,
A desert vast without a bound,
And nothing left to eat or drink,
And a dark desert all around.

The honey of her Infant lips,
The bread & wine of her sweet smile,
The wild game of her roving eye,
Does him to Infancy beguile;

For as he eats & drinks he grows
Younger & younger every day;
And on the desert wild they both
Wander in terror & dismay.

Like the wild Stag she flees away,
Her fear plants many a thicket wild;
While he pursues her night & day,
By various arts of Love beguil'd;

By various arts of Love & Hate,
Till the wide desart planted o'er
With Labyrinths of wayward Love,
Where roams the Lion, Wolf & Boar;

Till he becomes a wayward Babe,
And she a weeping Woman Old;
Then many a Lover wanders here,
The Sun & Stars are nearer roll'd,

The trees bring forth sweet Extacy
To all who in the desart roam,
Till many a City there is Built
And many a pleasant Shepherd's home.

But when they find the frowning Babe,
Terror strikes thro' the region wide:
They cry, 'the Babe! the Babe is Born!'
And flee away on every side.

For who dare touch the frowning form,
His arm is wither'd to its root;
Lions, Boars, Wolves, all howling flee,
And every Tree does shed its fruit.

And none can touch that frowning form,
Except it be a Woman Old;
She nails him down upon the Rock,
And all is done as I have told.

THE LAND OF DREAMS

'Awake, awake, my little Boy!
Thou wast thy Mother's only joy;
Why dost thou weep in thy gentle sleep?
Awake! thy Father does thee keep.'

'O what Land is the Land of Dreams?
What are its Mountains, & what are its Streams?
O Father! I saw my Mother there,
Among the Lillies by waters fair.

'Among the Lambs, clothed in white,
She walk'd with her Thomas in sweet delight.
I wept for joy, like a dove I mourn;
O when shall I again return?'

'Dear Child, I also by pleasant Streams
Have wander'd all Night in the Land of Dreams;
But tho' calm & warm the waters wide,
I could not get to the other side.'

'Father, O father! what do we here
In this Land of unbelief & fear?
The Land of Dreams is better far,
Above the light of the Morning Star.'

MARY

Sweet Mary, the first time she ever was there,
Came into the Ball room among the Fair;
The young Men & Maidens around her throng,
And these are the words upon every tongue:

'An Angel is here from the heavenly climes,
Or again does return the golden times;
Her eyes outshine every brilliant ray,
She opens her lips – 'tis the Month of May.'

Mary moves in soft beauty & conscious delight,
To augment with sweet smiles all the joys of the
    Night,
Nor once blushes to own to the rest of the Fair
That sweet Love & Beauty are worthy our care.

In the Morning the Villagers rose with delight,
And repeated with pleasure the joys of the night,
And Mary arose among Friends to be free,
But no Friend from henceforward thou, Mary, shalt
    see.

Some said she was proud, some call'd her a whore,
And some, when she passed by, shut to the door;
A damp cold came o'er her, her blushes all fled;
Her lillies & roses are blighted & shed.

'Oh why was I born with a different Face?
Why was I not born like this Envious Race?
Why did Heaven adorn me with bountiful hand,
And then set me down in an envious Land?

'To be weak as a Lamb & smooth as a Dove,
And not to raise Envy, is call'd Christian Love;
But if you raise Envy your Merit's to blame
For planting such spite in the weak & the tame.

'I will humble my Beauty, I will not dress fine,
I will keep from the Ball, & my Eyes shall not shine;
And if any Girl's Lover forsakes her for me
I'll refuse him my hand, & from Envy be free.'

She went out in Morning, attir'd plain & neat;
'Proud Mary's gone Mad,' said the Child in the Street;
She went out in Morning in plain neat attire,
And came home in Evening bespatter'd with mire.

She trembled & wept, sitting on the Bed side,
She forgot it was Night, & she trembled & cried;
She forgot it was Night, she forgot it was Morn,
Her soft Memory imprinted with Faces of Scorn;

With Faces of Scorn & with Eyes of Disdain
Like foul Fiends inhabiting Mary's mild Brain,
She remembers no Face like the Human Divine;
All Faces have Envy, sweet Mary, but thine;

And thine is a Face of sweet Love in despair,
And thine is a Face of mild sorrow & care,
And thine is a Face of wild terror & fear
That shall never be quiet till laid on its bier.

THE CRYSTAL CABINET

The Maiden caught me in the Wild,
Where I was dancing merrily;
She put me into her Cabinet,
And Lock'd me up with a golden Key.

This Cabinet is form'd of Gold
And Pearl & Crystal shining bright,
And within it opens into a World
And a little lovely Moony Night.

Another England there I saw,
Another London with its Tower,
Another Thames & other Hills,
And another pleasant Surrey Bower,

Another Maiden like herself,
Translucent, lovely, shining clear,
Threefold each in the other clos'd –
O what a pleasant trembling fear!

O what a smile! a threefold Smile
Fill'd me, that like a flame I burn'd;
I bent to Kiss the lovely Maid,
And found a Threefold Kiss return'd.

I strove to sieze the inmost Form
With ardor fierce & hands of flame,
But burst the Crystal Cabinet
And like a Weeping Babe became:

A weeping Babe upon the wild,
And weeping Woman pale reclin'd,
And in the outward air again
I fill'd with woes the passing Wind.

THE GREY MONK

'I die, I die!' the Mother said,
'My Children die for lack of Bread.
What more has the merciless Tyrant said?'
The Monk sat down on the Stony Bed.

The blood red ran from the Grey Monk's side,
His hands & feet were wounded wide,
His Body bent, his arms & knees
Like to the roots of ancient trees.

His eye was dry; no tear could flow:
A hollow groan first spoke his woe.
He trembled & shudder'd upon the Bed;
At length with a feeble cry he said:

'When God commanded this hand to write
In the studious hours of deep midnight,
He told me the writing I wrote should prove
The Bane of all that on Earth I lov'd.

'My Brother starv'd between two Walls,
His Children's Cry my Soul appalls;
I mock'd at the wrack & griding chain,
My bent body mocks their torturing pain.

'Thy Father drew his Sword in the North,
With his thousands strong he marched forth,
Thy Brother has arm'd himself in Steel,
To avenge the wrongs thy Children feel.

'But vain the Sword & vain the Bow,
They never can work War's overthrow.
The Hermit's Prayer & the Widow's tear
Alone can free the World from fear.

'For a Tear is an Intellectual Thing,
And a Sigh is the Sword of an Angel King,
And the bitter groan of the Martyr's woe
Is an arrow from the Almightie's Bow.

'The hand of Vengeance found the Bed
To which the Purple Tyrant fled;
The iron hand crush'd the Tyrant's head,
And became a Tyrant in his stead.'

AUGURIES OF INNOCENCE

To see a World in a Grain of Sand
And a Heaven in a Wild Flower,
Hold Infinity in the palm of your hand
And Eternity in an hour.

A Robin Red breast in a Cage
Puts all Heaven in a Rage.

A Dove house fill'd with Doves & Pigeons
Shudders Hell thro' all its regions.

A Dog starv'd at his Master's Gate
Predicts the ruin of the State.

A Horse misus'd upon the Road
Calls to Heaven for Human blood.

Each outcry of the hunted Hare
A fibre from the Brain does tear.

A Skylark wounded in the wing,
A Cherubim does cease to sing.

The Game Cock clip'd & arm'd for fight
Does the Rising Sun affright.

Every Wolf's & Lion's howl
Raises from Hell a Human Soul.

The wild Deer wand'ring here & there
Keeps the Human Soul from Care.

The Lamb misus'd breeds Public strife
And yet forgives the Butcher's Knife.

The Bat that flits at close of Eve
Has left the Brain that won't Believe.
The Owl that calls upon the Night
Speaks the Unbeliever's fright.

He who shall hurt the little Wren
Shall never be belov'd by Men.

He who the Ox to wrath has mov'd
Shall never be by Woman lov'd.

The wanton Boy that kills the Fly
Shall feel the Spider's enmity.

He who torments the Chafer's sprite
Weaves a Bower in endless Night.

The Catterpiller on the Leaf
Repeats to thee thy Mother's grief.

Kill not the Moth nor Butterfly
For the Last Judgment draweth nigh.

He who shall train the Horse to war
Shall never pass the Polar Bar.

The Beggar's Dog & Widow's Cat,
Feed them, & thou wilt grow fat.

The Gnat that sings his Summer's song
Poison gets from Slander's tongue.
The poison of the Snake & Newt
Is the sweat of Envy's Foot.
The Poison of the Honey Bee
Is the Artist's Jealousy.

The Prince's Robes & Beggar's Rags
Are Toadstools on the Miser's Bags.

A truth that's told with bad intent
Beats all the Lies you can invent.
It is right it should be so;
Man was made for Joy & Woe,
And when this we rightly know,
Thro' the World we safely go.

Joy & Woe are woven fine,
A Clothing for the Soul divine;
Under every grief & pine
Runs a joy with silken twine.

The Babe is more than Swadling Bands,
Throughout all these Human Lands;
Tools were made, & Born were hands,
Every Farmer Understands.

Every Tear from Every Eye
Becomes a Babe in Eternity;
This is caught by Females bright
And return'd to its own delight.

The Bleat, the Bark, Bellow & Roar
Are Waves that Beat on Heaven's Shore.

The Babe that weeps the Rod beneath
Writes Revenge in realms of Death.

The Beggar's Rags fluttering in Air
Does to Rags the Heavens tear.

The Soldier arm'd with Sword & Gun
Palsied strikes the Summer's Sun.

The poor Man's Farthing is worth more
Than all the Gold of Afric's Shore.

One Mite wrung from the Lab'rer's hands
Shall buy & sell the Miser's Lands
Or if protected from on high
Does that whole Nation sell & buy.

He who mocks the Infant's Faith
Shall be mock'd in Age & Death.
He who shall teach the Child to Doubt
The rotting Grave shall ne'er get out.
He who respects the Infant's faith
Triumphs over Hell & Death.

The Child's Toys & the Old Man's Reasons
Are the Fruits of the Two seasons.

The Questioner who sits so sly
Shall never know how to Reply.
He who replies to words of Doubt
Doth put the Light of Knowledge out.

The Strongest Poison ever known
Came from Cæsar's Laurel Crown.

Nought can deform the Human Race
Like to the Armour's iron brace.

When Gold & Gems adorn the Plow
To peaceful Arts shall Envy Bow.

A Riddle or the Cricket's Cry
Is to Doubt a fit Reply.

The Emmet's Inch & Eagle's Mile
Make Lame Philosophy to smile.

He who Doubts from what he sees
Will ne'er Believe, do what you Please.
If the Sun & Moon should doubt,
They'd immediately Go out.

To be in a Passion you Good may do,
But no Good if a Passion is in you.

The Whore & Gambler, by the State
Licenc'd, build that Nation's Fate.
The Harlot's cry from Street to Street
Shall weave Old England's winding Sheet.

The Winner's Shout, the Loser's Curse,
Dance before dead England's Hearse.

Every Night & every Morn
Some to Misery are Born.
Every Morn & every Night
Some are Born to sweet delight.
Some are Born to sweet delight,
Some are Born to Endless Night.

We are led to Believe a Lie
When we see not Thro' the Eye
Which was Born in a Night, to perish in a Night,
When the Soul Slept in Beams of Light.

God Appears, & God is Light
To those poor Souls who dwell in Night,
But does a Human Form Display
To those who Dwell in Realms of Day.

LONG JOHN BROWN & LITTLE MARY BELL

Little Mary Bell had a Fairy in a Nut,
Long John Brown had the Devil in his Gut;
Long John Brown lov'd Little Mary Bell,
And the Fairy drew the Devil into the Nut-shell.

Her Fairy Skip'd out & her Fairy Skip'd in;
He laugh'd at the Devil saying 'Love is a Sin.'
The Devil he raged & the Devil he was wroth,
And the Devil enter'd into the Young Man's broth.

He was soon in the Gut of the loving Young Swain,
For John eat & drank to drive away Love's pain;
But all he could do he grew thinner & thinner,
Tho' he eat & drank as much as ten Men for his dinner.

Some said he had a Wolf in his stomach day & night,
Some said he had the Devil, & they guess'd right;
The fairy skip'd about in his Glory, Joy & Pride,
And he laugh'd at the Devil till poor John Brown died.

Then the Fairy skip'd out of the old Nut-shell,
And woe & alack for Pretty Mary Bell!
For the Devil crept in where the Fairy skip'd out,
And there goes Miss Bell with her fusty old Nut.

WILLIAM BOND

I wonder whether the Girls are mad,
And I wonder whether they mean to kill,
And I wonder if William Bond will die,
For assuredly he is very ill.

He went to Church in a May morning,
Attended by Fairies, one, two, & three;
But the Angels of Providence drove them away,
And he return'd home in Misery.

He went not out to the Field nor Fold,
He went not out to the Village nor Town,
But he came home in a black black cloud,
And he took to his Bed, & there lay down.

And an Angel of Providence at his Feet,
And an Angel of Providence at his Head,
And in the midst a Black Black Cloud,
And in the midst the Sick Man on his Bed.

And on his Right hand was Mary Green,
And on his Left hand was his Sister Jane,
And their tears fell thro' the black black Cloud
To drive away the sick man's pain.

'O William, if thou dost another Love,
Dost another Love better than poor Mary,
Go & take that other to be thy Wife,
And Mary Green shall her Servant be.'

'Yes, Mary, I do another Love,
Another I Love far better than thee,
And Another I will have for my Wife;
Then what have I to do with thee?

'For thou art Melancholy Pale,
And on thy Head is the cold Moon's Shine,
But she is ruddy & bright as day,
And the sun beams dazzle from her eyne.'

Mary trembled & Mary chill'd,
And Mary fell down on the right hand floor.
That William Bond & his Sister Jane
Scarce could recover Mary more.

When Mary woke & found her Laid
On the Right hand of her William dear,
On the Right hand of his loved Bed,
And saw her William Bond so near,

The Fairies that fled from William Bond
Danced around her Shining Head;
They danced over the Pillow white,
And the Angels of Providence left the Bed.

I thought Love liv'd in the hot sun shine,
But O he lives in the Moony light!
I thought to find Love in the heat of day,
But sweet Love is the Comforter of Night.

Seek Love in the Pity of others' Woe,
In the gentle relief of another's care,
In the darkness of night & the winter's snow,
In the naked & outcast, Seek Love there.

POEMS FROM BLAKE'S MS. BOOK
(Commonly known as The 'Rossetti' MS.)

(About 1800–1803)

(The following verses exist only in MS., and were written, probably about the year 1800, in the early pages of what had been a sketch-book containing some seventy small drawings, similar in size and character to those of 'The Gates of Paradise', and about a dozen full-page illustrations. Blake had already used the other end of this book for the early versions of the 'Songs of Experience' and a little later he crowded the pages with prose comments, tags and quips on painting, which comprise the so-called 'Public Address', the more carefully written and more important paragraphs concerning his picture, 'The Last Judgment', the couplets of 'The Everlasting Gospel', and a number of hastily-written epigrams on friends and acquaintances.)

1

My Spectre around me night & day
Like a Wild beast guards my way;
My Emanation, far within,
Weeps incessantly for my Sin.

2

A Fathomless & boundless Deep
There we wander, there we weep;
On the hungry craving wind
My Spectre follows thee behind.

3

He scents thy footsteps in the snow
Wheresoever thou dost go
Thro' the wintry hail & rain:
When wilt thou return again?

4

Dost thou not in Pride & scorn
Fill with tempests all my morn?
And with jealousies & fears
Fill my pleasant nights with tears?

Seven of my sweet loves thy knife
Has bereaved of their life;
Their marble tombs I built with tears
And with cold & shuddering fears.

6

Seven more loves weep night & day
Round the tombs where my loves lay,
And seven more loves attend each night
Around my couch with torches bright.

7

And Seven more Loves in my bed
Crown with wine my mournful head,
Pitying & forgiving all
Thy transgressions great & small.

8

When wilt thou return & view
My loves, & them to life renew?
When wilt thou return & live?
When wilt thou pity, as I forgive?

9

'Never, Never I return!
Still for Victory I burn:
Living, thee alone I'll have,
And when dead I'll be thy Grave.

10

'Thro' the Heav'n & Earth & Hell
Thou shalt never, never quell;
I will fly & thou pursue,
Night & Morn the flight renew.'

11

Till I turn from Female Love
And root up the Infernal Grove,
I shall never worthy be
To Step into Eternity.

12

And to end thy cruel mocks
Annihilate thee on the rocks,
And another form create
To be subservient to my Fate.

13

Let us agree to give up Love
And root up the infernal grove;
Then we shall return & see
The worlds of happy Eternity.

14

& Throughout all Eternity
I forgive you, you forgive me;
As our dear Redeemer said,
'This the Wine & this the Bread.'

Mock on, Mock on! Voltaire, Rousseau,
Mock on, Mock on! 'tis all in vain!
You throw the sand against the wind,
And the wind blows it back again.

And every sand becomes a Gem
Reflected in the beams divine;
Blown back they blind the mocking Eye,
But still in Israel's paths they shine.

The Atoms of Democritus
And Newton's Particles of Light
Are sands upon the Red sea shore
Where Israel's tents do shine so bright.

MORNING

To find the Western path
Right thro' the Gates of Wrath
I urge my way.
Sweet Mercy leads me on,
With soft repentant moan
I see the break of day.

The war of swords & spears
Melted by dewy tears
Exhales on high.
The Sun is freed from fears
And with soft grateful tears
Ascends the sky.

THE BIRDS

He. Where thou dwellest, in what grove,
      Tell me, Fair one, tell me love
      Where thou thy charming Nest doth build,
      O thou pride of every field!

She. Yonder stands a lonely tree,
      There I live & mourn for thee:
      Morning drinks my silent tear,
      And evening winds my sorrows bear.

He. O thou Summer's harmony,
      I have liv'd & mourn'd for thee:
      Each day I mourn along the wood,
      And night hath heard my sorrows loud.

She. Dost thou truly long for me?
      And am I thus sweet to thee?
      Sorrow now is at an End,
      O My Lover & my Friend!

He. Come, on wings of joy we'll fly
      To where my Bower hangs on high;
      Come & make thy calm retreat
      Among green leaves & blossoms sweet.

Why was Cupid a Boy
And why a boy was he?
He should have been a Girl
For ought that I can see;

For he shoots with his bow,
And the Girl shoots with her Eye;
And they both are merry & glad,
And laugh when we do cry.

And to make Cupid a Boy
Was the Cupid Girl's mocking plan;
For a boy can't interpret the thing
Till he is become a man;

And then he's so pierc'd with cares
And wounded with arrowy smarts
That the whole business of his life
Is to pick out the heads of the darts.

'Twas the Greeks' love of war
Turn'd Love into a Boy
And Woman into a Statue of Stone,
And away fled every Joy.

I rose up at the dawn of day:
'Get thee away, get thee away!
Pray'st thou for Riches? away, away!
This is the Throne of Mammon grey.'

Said I: 'this sure is very odd,
I took it to be the Throne of God,
For every Thing besides I have,
It is only for Riches that I can crave.

'I have Mental Joy & Mental Health,
And Mental Friends & Mental wealth;
I've a Wife I love & that loves me;
I've all But Riches Bodily.

'I am in God's presence night & day,
And he never turns his face away.
The accuser of sins by my side does stand,
And he holds my money bag in his hand.

'For my worldly things God makes him pay,
And he'd pay for more if to him I would pray,
And so you may do the worst you can do,
Be assur'd Mr. Devil, I won't pray to you.

'Then If for Riches I must not Pray,
God knows I little of Prayers need say;
So, as a Church is known by its Steeple,
If I pray it must be for other People.

'He says if I do not worship him for a God
I shall eat coarser food & go worse shod;
So, as I don't value such things as these,
You must do, Mr. Devil, just as God please.'

TWO POEMS
from Blake's letters to Thomas Butts

(1800 & 1802)
I
To my Friend Butts I write
My first Vision of Light,
On the yellow sands sitting.
The Sun was Emitting
His Glorious beams
From Heaven's high Streams.
Over Sea, over Land
My Eyes did Expand
Into regions of air
Away from all Care,
Into regions of fire
Remote from Desire.
The Light of the Morning
Heaven's Mountains adorning,
In particles bright
The jewels of Light
Distinct shone & clear.
Amaz'd & in fear
I each particle gazed,
Astonish'd, amazed;

For each was a Man
Human form'd. Swift I ran,
For they beckon'd to me
Remote by the Sea,
Saying: 'Each grain of Sand,
Every stone on the Land,
Each rock & each hill,
Each fountain & rill,
Each herb & each tree,
Mountain, hill, earth & sea,
Cloud, Meteor & Star,
Are Men Seen Afar.'
I stood in the Streams
Of Heaven's bright beams
And Saw Felpham sweet
Beneath my bright feet
In soft Female charms,
And in her fair arms
My Shadow I knew,
And my wife's shadow too,
And My Sister, & Friend.
We like Infants descend
In our Shadows on Earth,
Like a weak mortal birth.
My Eyes, more & more,

Like a Sea without Shore,
Continue expanding,
The Heavens commanding,
Till the Jewels of Light,
Heavenly Men beaming bright,
Appear'd as One Man
Who Complacent began
My limbs to infold
In his beams of bright gold.
Like dross purg'd away
All my mire & my clay:
Soft consum'd in delight,
In his bosom Sun bright
I remain'd. Soft he smil'd,
And I heard his voice Mild
Saying: 'This is My Fold,
O thou Ram horn'd with gold,
Who awakest from Sleep
On the Sides of the Deep.
On the Mountains around
The roarings resound
Of the lion & wolf,
The loud sea & deep gulf:
These are guards of My Fold,
O thou Ram horn'd with gold.'
And the voice faded mild,
I remain'd as a Child,

All I ever had known
Before me bright shone,
I saw you & your wife
By the fountains of life.
Such the Vision to me
Appear'd on the Sea.

Felpham,
Oct. 24 1800.

II

With happiness stretch'd across the hills
In a cloud that dewy sweetness distills,
With a blue sky spread over with wings,
And a mild sun that mounts & sings,
With trees & fields full of Fairy elves,
And little devils who fight for themselves –
Rememb'ring the Verses that Hayley sung
When my heart knock'd against the root of my tongue,
With Angels planted in Hawthorn bowers,
And God himself in the passing hours,
With Silver Angels across my way
And Golden Demons that none can stay,
With my Father hovering upon the wind
And my Brother Robert just behind,
And my Brother John, the evil one,
In a black cloud making his mone –
Tho' dead, they appear upon my path,
Notwithstanding my terrible wrath

143

They beg, they intreat, they drop their tears,
Fill'd full of hopes, fill'd full of fears –
With a thousand Angels upon the Wind,
Pouring disconsolate from behind
To drive them off, & before my way
A frowning Thistle implores my stay.

What to others a trifle appears
Fills me full of smiles or tears;
For double the vision my Eyes do see,
And a double vision is always with me.
With my inward Eye, 'tis an old Man grey,
With my outward, a Thistle across my way.

'If thou goest back,' the thistle said,
'Thou art to endless woe betray'd;
For here does Theotormon lower,
And here is Enitharmon's bower,
And Los the terrible thus hath sworn,
Because thou backward dost return,
Poverty, Envy, old age & fear
Shall bring thy Wife upon a bier,
And Butts shall give what Fuseli gave,
A dark black Rock & a gloomy Cave.'

I struck the Thistle with my foot
And broke him up from his delving root.
'Must the duties of life each other cross?
Must every joy be dung & dross?
Must my dear Butts feel cold neglect
Because I give Hayley his due respect?
Must Flaxman look upon me as wild
And all my friends be with doubts beguil'd?
Must my Wife live in my Sister's bane,
Or my Sister survive on my Love's pain?
The curses of Los, the terrible shade,
And his dismal terrors make me afraid.'

So I spoke, & struck in my wrath
The old man weltering upon my path.
Then Los appear'd in all his power:
In the Sun he appear'd, descending before
My face in fierce flames; in my double sight
'Twas outward a Sun, inward Los in his might.

'My hands are labour'd day & night,
And Ease comes never in my sight.
My Wife has no indulgence given
Except what comes to her from heaven.
We eat little, we drink less,
This Earth breeds not our happiness.
Another Sun feeds our life's streams,

We are not warmed with thy beams;
Thou measurest not the Time to me,
Nor yet the Space that I do see;
My Mind is not with thy light array'd,
Thy Terrors shall not make me afraid.'

When I had my Defiance given,
The Sun stood trembling in heaven,
The Moon, that glow'd remote below,
Became leprous & white as snow,
And every soul of men on the Earth
Felt affliction & sorrow & sickness & dearth.
Los flam'd in my path, & the Sun was hot
With the bows of my Mind & the arrows of Thought.
My bowstring fierce with ardour breathes,
My arrows glow in their golden sheaves,
My brothers & father march before,
The heavens drop with human gore.

Now I a fourfold vision see,
And a fourfold vision is given to me;
'Tis fourfold in my supreme delight
And threefold in soft Beulah's night
And twofold Always. May God us keep
From single vision & Newton's sleep.

Felpham,
Nov. 22: 1802.

THE EVERLASTING GOSPEL
Passages collected chiefly from the MS. Book.

There is not one Moral Virtue that Jesus Inculcated
but Plato & Cicero did Inculcate before him: what then
did Christ Inculcate? Forgiveness of Sins. This alone
is the Gospel, and this is the Life & Immortality
brought to light by Jesus, Even the Covenant of
Jehovah, which is This: If you forgive one another
your Trespasses, so shall Jehovah forgive you, That he
himself may dwell among you; but if you Avenge, you
Murder the Divine Image, & he cannot dwell among
you because you Murder him: he arises again & you
deny that he is Arisen & are blind to Spirit.

(*About* 1818)
If Moral Virtue was Christianity
Christ's Pretensions were all Vanity,
And Caiaphas & Pilate, Men
Praise Worthy, & the Lion's Den
And not the Sheepfold, Allegories
Of God & Heaven & their Glories.
The Moral Christian is the Cause
Of the Unbeliever & his Laws.
The Roman Virtues, Warlike Fame,
Take Jesus' & Jehovah's Name:
For what is Antichrist but those

Who against Sinners Heaven close
With Iron bars, in Virtuous State,
And Rhadamanthus at the Gate?
What can this Gospel of Jesus be?
What Life & Immortality,
What was it that he brought to Light
That Plato & Cicero did not write?
The Heathen Deities wrote them all,
These Moral Virtues, great & small.
What is the Accusation of Sin
But Moral Virtue's deadly Gin?
The Moral Virtues in their Pride
Did o'er the World triumphant ride
In Wars & Sacrifice for Sin,
And Souls to Hell ran trooping in.
The Accuser, Holy God of All
This Pharisaic Worldly Ball,
Amidst them in his Glory Beams
Upon the Rivers & the Streams.
Then Jesus rose & said to Me,
'Thy Sins are all forgiven thee.'
Loud Pilate Howl'd, loud Caiaphas yell'd
When they the Gospel Light beheld.
It was when Jesus said to Me
'Thy Sins are all forgiven thee'
The Christian trumpets loud proclaim

Thro' all the World in Jesus' name
Mutual forgiveness of each Vice
And oped the Gates of Paradise.
The Moral Virtues in Great fear
Formed the Cross & Nails & Spear,
And the Accuser standing by
Cried out, 'Crucify! Crucify!
Our Moral Virtues ne'er can be,
Nor Warlike pomp & Majesty,
For Moral Virtues all begin
In the Accusations of Sin,
And all the Heroic Virtues End
In destroying the Sinners' Friend.
Am I not Lucifer the Great,
And you, my daughters in Great State,
The fruit of my Mysterious Tree
Of Good & Evil, & Misery
And Death & Hell which now begin
On everyone who Forgives Sin?'

Was Jesus Humble, or did he
Give any Proofs of Humility?
Boast of high Things with Humble tone,
And give with Charity a Stone?
When but a Child he ran away,
And left his Parents in dismay.

When they had wander'd three days long
These were the words upon his tongue:
'No Earthly Parents I confess:
I am doing my Father's business.'
When the rich learned Pharisee
Came to consult him secretly,
Upon his heart with Iron pen
He wrote, 'Ye must be born again.'
He was too proud to take a bribe;
He spoke with authority, not like a Scribe.
He says, with most consummate Art,
'Follow me, I am meek & lowly of heart,'
As that is the only way to escape
The Miser's net & the Glutton's trap.
He who loves his Enemies betrays his Friends:
This surely is not what Jesus intends,
But the sneaking Pride of Heroic Schools,
And the Scribes' & Pharisees' Virtuous Rules;
For he acts with honest, triumphant Pride,
And this is the cause that Jesus died.
He did not die with Christian Ease,
Asking pardon of his Enemies:
If he had, Caiaphas would forgive:
Sneaking submission can always live.
He had only to say that God was the devil,
And the devil was God, like a Christian Civil,
Mild Christian regrets to the devil confess

For affronting him thrice in the Wilderness,
He had soon been bloody Cæsar's Elf,
And at last he would have been Cæsar himself,
Like Dr. Priestly & Bacon & Newton –
Poor Spiritual Knowledge is not worth a button –
For thus the Gospel Sir Isaac confutes:
'God can only be known by his Attributes,
And as to the Indwelling of the Holy Ghost
Or of Christ & his Father, it's all a boast
And Pride & Vanity of the imagination
That disdains to follow this World's Fashion.'
To teach Doubt & Experiment
Certainly was not what Christ meant.
What was he doing all that time,
From twelve years old to manly prime?
Was he then Idle, or the Less
About his Father's business?
Or was his wisdom held in scorn
Before his wrath began to burn
In Miracles throughout the Land,
That quite unnerv'd the haughty hand?
If he had been Antichrist, Creeping Jesus,
He'd have done any thing to please us:
Gone sneaking into Synagogues,
And not us'd the Elders & Priests like dogs,
But Humble as a Lamb or Ass
Obey'd himself to Caiaphas.

God wants not Man to Humble himself:
This is the trick of the ancient Elf.
This is the Race that Jesus ran:
Humble to God, Haughty to Man,
Cursing the Rulers before the People
Even to the temple's highest Steeple,
And when he Humbled himself to God
Then descended the Cruel Rod.
'If thou humblest thyself, thou humblest me:
Thou also dwell'st in Eternity.
Thou art a Man, God is no more;
Thy own humanity learn to adore,
For that is my Spirit of Life,
Awake, arise to Spiritual Strife,
And thy Revenge abroad display
In terrors at the Last Judgment day.
God's Mercy & Long Suffering
Is but the Sinner to Judgment to bring.
Thou on the Cross for them shalt pray,
And take Revenge at the Last Day.'
Jesus replied, & thunders hurl'd:
'I never will Pray for the World.
Once I did so when I pray'd in the Garden:
I wish'd to take with me a Bodily Pardon.'
Can that which was of woman born,
In the absence of the Morn,
When the Soul fell into Sleep,

And Archangels round it weep,
Shooting out against the Light
Fibres of a deadly night,
Reasoning upon its own dark Fiction,
In Doubt which is Self Contradiction?
Humility is only doubt,
And does the Sun & Moon blot out,
Rooting over with thorns & stems
The buried Soul & all its gems.
This Life's five Windows of the Soul
Distorts the Heavens from Pole to Pole
And leads you to Believe a Lie
When you see with, not thro' the Eye
That was born in a night, to perish in a night,
When the Soul slept in the beams of Light.
Was Jesus Chaste, or did he
Give any Lessons of Chastity?
The morning blush'd fiery red:
Mary was found in Adulterous bed;
Earth groan'd beneath, & Heaven above
Trembled at discovery of Love.
Jesus was sitting in Moses' Chair,
They brought the trembling Woman There.
Moses commands she be ston'd to death:
What was the sound of Jesus' breath?
He laid His hand on Moses' Law;
The Ancient Heavens, in Silent Awe,

Writ with Curses from Pole to Pole,
All away began to roll.
The Earth, trembling & Naked lay
In secret bed of Mortal Clay,
On Sinai felt the hand divine
Putting back the bloody shrine,
And She heard the breath of God
As She heard by Eden's flood,
'Good & Evil are no more!
Sinai's trumpets, cease to roar!
Cease, finger of God, to write!
The Heavens are not clean in thy Sight.
Thou art Good, & thou Alone;
Nor may the sinner cast one stone.
To be Good only is to be
A God or else a Pharisee.
Thou Angel of the Presence Divine,
That didst create this Body of Mine,
Wherefore hast thou writ these Laws
And Created Hell's dark jaws?
My Presence I will take from thee:
A Cold Leper thou shalt be.
Tho' thou wast so pure & bright
That Heaven was Impure in thy Sight,
Tho' thy Oath turn'd Heaven Pale,
Tho' thy Covenant built Hell's Jail,
Tho' thou didst all to Chaos roll

With the Serpent for its soul,
Still the breath Divine does move,
And the breath Divine is Love.
Mary, Fear Not. Let me see
The Seven Devils that torment thee:
Hide not from my Sight thy Sin,
That forgiveness thou maist win.
Has no Man Condemned thee?'
'No Man, Lord.' 'then what is he
Who shall Accuse thee? Come Ye forth,
Fallen fiends of Heav'nly birth
That have forgot your Ancient love
And driven away my trembling Dove.
You shall bow before her feet;
You shall lick the dust for Meat;
And tho' you cannot Love, but Hate,
Shall be beggars at Love's Gate.
What was thy love? let me see it;
Was it love or dark deceit?'
'Love too long from Me has fled;
'Twas dark deceit, to Earn my bread;
'Twas Covet, or 'twas Custom, or
Some trifle not worth caring for;
That they may call a shame & Sin
Love's temple that God dwelleth in,
And hide in secret hidden shrine
The Naked Human form divine,

And render that a Lawless thing
On which the Soul Expands its wing,
But this, O Lord, this was my Sin
When first I let these devils in:
In dark pretence to Chastity
Blaspheming Love, blaspheming thee.
Thence Rose Secret Adulteries,
And thence did Covet also rise.
My Sin thou hast forgiven me,
Canst thou forgive my Blasphemy?
Canst thou return to this dark Hell,
And in my burning bosom dwell?
And canst thou die that I may live?
And canst thou Pity & forgive?'
Then Roll'd the Shadowy Man away
From the Limbs of Jesus, to make them his prey,
An Ever devouring appetite,
Glittering with festering venoms bright;
Crying 'Crucify this cause of distress,
Who don't keep the secrets of holiness!
All Mental Powers by Diseases we bind,
But he heals the deaf & the dumb & the Blind.
Whom God has afflicted for Secret Ends,
He Comforts & Heals & calls them Friends.'
But when Jesus was Crucified,
Then was perfected his glitt'ring pride.
In three Nights he devour'd his prey,

And still he devours the Body of Clay;
For Dust & Clay is the Serpent's meat,
Which never was made for Man to Eat.
Seeing this False Christ, In Fury & Passion
I made my Voice heard all over the Nation.
What are those, &c.

Was Jesus gentle, or did he
Give any marks of Gentility?
When twelve years old he ran away
And left his Parents in dismay.
When after three days' sorrow found,
Loud as Sinai's trumpet sound:
'No Earthly Parents I confess
My Heavenly Father's business.
Ye understand not what I say,
And angry, force me to obey.'
Obedience is a duty then,
And favour gains with God & Men.
John from the Wilderness loud cried;
Satan gloried in his Pride.
'Come,' said Satan, 'come away,
I'll soon see if you'll obey!
John for disobedience bled,
But you can turn the stones to bread.
God's high king & God's high Priest
Shall Plant their Glories in your breast
If Caiaphas you will obey,

157

If Herod you with bloody Prey
Feed with the Sacrifice, & be
Obedient, fall down, worship me.'
Thunders & lightnings broke around,
And Jesus' voice in thunders' sound:
'Thus I sieze the Spiritual Prey:
Ye smiters with disease, make way!
I come Your King & God to sieze,
Is God a Smiter with disease?'
The God of this World rag'd in vain.
He bound Old Satan in his Chain,
And bursting forth, his furious ire
Became a Chariot of fire:
Throughout the land he took his course,
And traced diseases to their Source:
He curs'd the Scribe and Pharisee,
Trampling down Hipocrisy:
Where'er his Chariot took its way
There Gates of death let in the day,
Broke down from every Chain & Bar,
And Satan in his Spiritual War
Drag'd at his Chariot wheels: loud howl'd
The God of this World: louder roll'd
The Chariot Wheels, & louder still
His voice was heard from Zion's hill,
And in his hand the Scourge shone bright;
He scourg'd the Merchant Canaanite

From out the Temple of his Mind,
And in his Body tight does bind
Satan & all his Hellish Crew;
And thus with wrath he did subdue
The Serpent Bulk of Nature's dross,
Till he had nail'd it to the Cross.
He took on Sin in the Virgin's Womb
And put it off on the Cross & Tomb
To be Worship'd by the Church of Rome.

Was Jesus Born of a Virgin Pure
With narrow Soul & looks demure?
If he intended to take on Sin
The Mother should an Harlot been,
Just such a one as Magdalen
With seven devils in her Pen:
Or were Jew Virgins still more Curst,
And more sucking devils nurst?
Or what was it which he took on
That he might bring Salvation?
A Body subject to be Tempted,
From neither pain nor grief exempted;
Or such a body as might not feel
The passions that with Sinners deal?
Yes, but they say he never fell.
Ask Caiaphas, for he can tell.
'He mock'd the Sabbath, & he mock'd

The Sabbath's God, & he unlock'd
The Evil spirits from their Shrines,
And turn'd Fishermen to Divines;
O'erturn'd the Tent of Secret Sins,
& its Golden cords & Pins:
'Tis the Bloody Shrine of War
Pinn'd around from Star to Star:
Halls of justice, hating Vice,
Where the devil Combs his lice:
He turn'd the devils into Swine
That he might tempt the Jews to dine;
Since which, a Pig has got a look
That for a Jew may be mistook.
'Obey your parents.' – what says he?
'Woman, what have I to do with thee?
No Earthly Parents I confess:
I am doing my Father's Business.'
He scorn'd Earth's Parents, scorn'd Earth's God,
And mock'd the one & the other's Rod;
His Seventy Disciples sent
Against Religion & Government:
They by the Sword of Justice fell,
And him their Cruel Murderer tell.
He left his Father's trade to roam,
A wand'ring Vagrant without Home;
And thus he other's labour stole,
That he might live above Controll.

The Publicans & Harlots he
Selected for his Company,
And from the Adulteress turn'd away
God's righteous Law, that lost its Prey.'

The Vision of Christ that thou dost see
Is my Vision's Greatest Enemy:
Thine has a great hook nose like thine,
Mine has a snub nose like to mine:
Thine is the friend of All Mankind,
Mine speaks in parables to the Blind.
Thine loves the same world that mine hates,
Thy Heaven doors are my Hell Gates.
Socrates taught what Meletus
Loath'd as a Nation's bitterest Curse,
And Caiaphas was in his own Mind
A benefactor to Mankind.
Both read the Bible day & night,
But thou read'st black where I read white.

THERE IS NO NATURAL RELIGION

(1788)

[a]

The Argument

Man has no notion of moral fitness but from Education. Naturally he is only a natural organ subject to Sense.

I

Man cannot naturally Percieve but through his natural or bodily organs.

II

Man by his reasoning power can only compare & judge of what he has already perceiv'd.

III

From a perception of only 3 senses or 3 elements none could deduce a fourth or fifth.

IV

None could have other than natural or organic thoughts if he had none but organic perceptions.

V

Man's desires are limited by his perceptions: none can desire what he has not perciev'd.

VI

The desires & perceptions of man untaught by any thing but organs of sense, must be limited to objects of sense.

Conclusion

If it were not for the Poetic or Prophetic Character, the Philosophic & Experimental would soon be at the ratio of all things & stand still, unable to do other than repeat the same dull round over again.

[*b*]
I

Man's perceptions are not bounded by organs of perception: he percieves more than sense (tho' ever so acute) can discover.

II

Reason, or the ratio of all we have already known, is not the same that it shall be when we know more.

III
[This proposition is missing.]

IV

The bounded is loathed by its possessor. The same dull round, even of a universe, would soon become a mill with complicated wheels.

V

If the many become the same as the few when possess'd, More! More! is the cry of a mistaken soul: less than All cannot satisfy Man.

VI

If any could desire what he is incapable of possessing, despair must be his eternal lot.

VII

The desire of Man being Infinite, the possession is Infinite & himself Infinite.

Application

He who sees the Infinite in all things, sees God. He who sees the Ratio only, sees himself only.

Therefore God becomes as we are, that we may be as he is.

ALL RELIGIONS ARE ONE

(1788)

The Voice of one crying in the Wilderness.

The Argument
As the true method of knowledge is experiment, the true faculty of knowing must be the faculty which experiences. This faculty I treat of.

Principle 1st
That the Poetic Genius is the true Man, and that the body or outward form of Man is derived from the Poetic Genius. Likewise that the forms of all things are derived from their Genius, which by the Ancients was call'd an Angel & Spirit & Demon.

Principle 2d
As all men are alike in outward form, So (and with the same infinite variety) all are alike in the Poetic Genius.

Principle 3d
No man can think, write, or speak from his heart, but he must intend truth. Thus all sects of Philosophy are from the Poetic Genius adapted to the weaknesses of every individual.

Principle 4

As none by traveling over known lands can find out the unknown, So, from already acquired knowledge, Man could not acquire more; therefore an universal Poetic Genius exists.

Principle 5

The Religions of all Nations are derived from each Nation's different reception of the Poetic Genius, which is every where call'd the Spirit of Prophecy.

Principle 6

The Jewish & Christian Testaments are An original derivation from the Poetic Genius: this is necessary from the confined nature of bodily sensation.

Principle 7

As all men are alike (tho' infinitely various), So all Religions, &, as all similars, have one source.

The true Man is the source, he being the Poetic Genius.

From MILTON
A POEM IN TWO BOOKS
To Justify the Ways of God to Men

(*Begun* 1804)

PREFACE

The Stolen and Perverted Writings of Homer & Ovid,
of Plato & Cicero, which all Men ought to contemn,
are set up by artifice against the Sublime of the Bible;
but when the New Age is at leisure to Pronounce, all
will be set right, & those Grand Works of the more
ancient & consciously & professedly Inspired Men will
hold their proper rank, & the Daughters of Memory
shall become the Daughters of Inspiration. Shakspeare
& Milton were both curb'd by the general malady &
infection from the silly Greek & Latin slaves of the
Sword.

Rouze up, O Young Men of the New Age! set your
foreheads against the ignorant Hirelings! For we have
Hirelings in the Camp, the Court & the University,
who would, if they could, for ever depress Mental &
prolong Corporeal War. Painters! on you I call.
Sculptors! Architects! Suffer not the fashionable Fools
to depress your powers by the prices they pretend to
give for contemptible works, or the expensive adver-
tizing boasts that they make of such works: believe
Christ & his Apostles that there is a Class of Men

whose whole delight is in Destroying. We do not want either Greek or Roman Models if we are but just & true to our own Imaginations, those Worlds of Eternity in which we shall live for ever in Jesus our Lord.

And did those feet in ancient time
Walk upon England's mountains green:
And was the holy Lamb of God
On England's pleasant pastures seen!

And did the Countenance Divine
Shine forth upon our clouded hills?
And was Jerusalem builded here
Among these dark Satanic Mills?

Bring me my Bow of burning gold:
Bring me my Arrows of desire:
Bring me my Spear: O clouds unfold!
Bring me my Chariot of fire!

I will not cease from Mental Fight,
Nor shall my Sword sleep in my hand
Till we have built Jerusalem
In England's green & pleasant Land.

Would to God that all the Lord's people were Prophets.

Numbers xi, Ch. 29 v.

THE BOOK OF THEL

(1789)

THEL'S Motto

Does the Eagle know what is in the pit?
Or wilt thou go ask the Mole:
Can Wisdom be put in a silver rod?
Or Love in a golden bowl?

I

The daughters of Mne Seraphim led round their sunny
    flocks,
All but the youngest: she in paleness sought the secret
    air,
To fade away like morning beauty from her mortal
    day;
Down by the river of Adona her soft voice is heard,
And thus her gentle lamentation falls like morning
    dew:

'O life of this our spring! why fades the lotus of the
    water?
Why fade these children of the spring? born but to
    smile & fall.
Ah! Thel is like a wąt'ry bow, and like a parting cloud,
Like a reflection in a glass, like shadows in the water,

Like dreams of infants, like a smile upon an infant's
    face,
Like the dove's voice, like transient day, like music in
    the air.
Ah! gentle may I lay me down and gentle rest my head,
And gentle sleep the sleep of death, and gentle hear the
    voice
Of him that walketh in the garden in the evening time.'

The Lilly of the Valley, breathing in the humble grass,
Answer'd the lovely maid and said: 'I am a wat'ry
    weed,
And I am very small and love to dwell in lowly vales,
So weak the gilded butterfly scarce perches on my
    head;

Yet I am visited from heaven, and he that smiles on all
Walks in the valley, and each morn over me spreads his
    hand
Saying, "rejoice, thou humble grass, thou new-born
    lilly flower,
Thou gentle maid of silent valleys and of modest
    brooks;
For thou shalt be clothed in light, and fed with
    morning manna,
Till summer's heat melts thee beside the fountains and
    the springs

To flourish in eternal vales": then why should Thel
    complain?
Why should the mistress of the vales of Har utter a
    sigh?'

She ceas'd & smil'd in tears, then sat down in her silver
    shrine.

Thel answer'd: 'O thou little virgin of the peaceful
    valley,
Giving to those that cannot crave, the voiceless, the
    o'ertired;
Thy breath doth nourish the innocent lamb, he smells
    thy milky garments,
He crops thy flowers while thou sittest smiling in his
    face,
Wiping his mild and meekin mouth from all
    contagious taints.
Thy wine doth purify the golden honey; thy perfume,
Which thou dost scatter on every little blade of grass
    that springs,
Revives the milked cow, & tames the fire-breathing
    steed.
But Thel is like a faint cloud kindled at the rising sun:
I vanish from my pearly throne, and who shall find my
    place?'

'Queen of the vales,' the Lilly answer'd, 'ask the tender
    cloud
And it shall tell thee why it glitters in the morning sky,
And why it scatters its bright beauty thro' the humid
    air.
Descend, O little cloud, & hover before the eyes of
    Thel.'

The Cloud descended, and the Lilly bow'd her modest
    head
And went to mind her numerous charge among the
    verdant grass.

II

'O little Cloud,' the virgin said, 'I charge thee tell to me
Why thou complainest not when in one hour thou fade
    away:
Then we shall seek thee, but not find: ah! Thel is like
    to thee:
I pass away: yet I complain, and no one hears my
    voice.'

The Cloud then shew'd his golden head & his bright
    form emerg'd.
Hovering and glittering on the air before the face of
    Thel.

'O virgin, know'st thou not, our steeds drink of the
    golden springs
Where Luvah doth renew his horses: look'st thou on
    my youth,
And fearest thou, because I vanish and am seen no
    more,
Nothing remains? O maid, I tell thee, when I pass
    away,
It is to tenfold life, to love, to peace, and raptures holy
Unseen descending weigh my light wings upon balmy
    flowers
And court the fair eyed dew to take me to her shining
    tent:
The weeping virgin, trembling kneels before the risen
    sun,
Till we arise, link'd in a golden band, and never part,
But walk united, bearing food to all our tender
    flowers.'

'Dost thou, O little Cloud? I fear that I am not like
    thee,
For I walk thro' the vales of Har, and smell the
    sweetest flowers,
But I feed not the little flowers. I hear the warbling
    birds,
But I feed not the warbling birds: they fly and seek
    their food:

But Thel delights in these no more, because I fade
    away;
And all shall say, "without a use this shining woman
    liv'd,
Or did she only live to be at death the food of
    worms?" '

The Cloud reclin'd upon his airy throne and answer'd
    thus:

'Then if thou art the food of worms, O virgin of the
    skies,
How great thy use, how great thy blessing! every
    thing that lives
Lives not alone, nor for itself: fear not, and I will call
The weak worm from its lowly bed, and thou shalt hear
    its voice.
Come forth, worm of the silent valley, to thy pensive
    queen.'

The helpless worm arose and sat upon the Lilly's leaf,
And the bright Cloud sail'd on, to find his partner in
    the vale.

III

Then Thel astonish'd view'd the Worm upon its dewy
     bed.

'Art thou a Worm? image of weakness, art thou but a
     Worm?
I see thee like an infant wrapped in the Lilly's leaf.
Ah, weep not, little voice, thou canst not speak, but
     thou canst weep.
Is this a Worm? I see thee lay helpless & naked,
     weeping
And none to answer, none to cherish thee with
     mother's smiles.'

The Clod of Clay heard the Worm's voice & rais'd her
     pitying head.
She bow'd over the weeping infant, and her life exhal'd
In milky fondness: then on Thel she fix'd her humble
     eyes.

'O beauty of the vales of Har, we live not for ourselves.
Thou seest me the meanest thing, and so I am indeed:
My bosom of itself is cold and of itself is dark,
But he that loves the lowly, pours his oil upon my head
And kisses me, and binds his nuptial bands around my
     breast,

And says: "Thou mother of my children, I have loved
    thee,
And I have given thee a crown that none can take
    away."
But how this is, sweet maid, I know not, and I cannot
    know;
I ponder, and I cannot ponder; yet I live and love.'

   The daughter of beauty wip'd her pitying tears with
    her white veil,
And said, 'Alas! I knew not this, and therefore did I
    weep.
That God would love a Worm I knew, and punish the
    evil foot
That wilful bruis'd its helpless form; but that he
    cherish'd it
With milk and oil I never knew, and therefore did I
    weep;
And I complain'd in the mild air, because I fade away
And lay me down in thy cold bed, and leave my shining
    lot.'

'Queen of the vales,' the matron Clay answer'd, 'I heard
    thy sighs,
And all thy moans flew o'er my roof, but I have call'd
    them down.
Wilt thou, O Queen, enter my house? 'tis given thee to
    enter
And to return: fear nothing, enter with thy virgin feet.'

IV

The eternal gates' terrific porter lifted the northern
    bar.
Thel enter'd in & saw the secrets of the land unknown.
She saw the couches of the dead, & where the fibrous
    roots
Of every heart on earth infixes deep its restless twists:
A land of sorrows & of tears where never smile was
    seen.

She wander'd in the land of clouds thro' valleys dark,
    list'ning
Dolours and lamentations; waiting oft beside a dewy
    grave
She stood in silence, list'ning to the voices of the
    ground,
Till to her own grave plot she came, & there she sat
    down,
And heard this voice of sorrow breathed from the
    hollow pit:

'Why cannot the Ear be closed to its own destruction?
Or the glist'ning Eye to the poison of a smile!
Why are Eyelids stor'd with arrows ready drawn,
Where a thousand fighting men in ambush lie,
Or an Eye of gifts & graces show'ring fruits & coined
    gold?
Why a Tongue impress'd with honey from every
    wind?
Why an Ear, a whirlpool fierce to draw creations in?
Why a Nostril wide inhaling terror trembling &
    affright?
Why a tender curb upon the youthful burning boy?
Why a little curtain of flesh on the bed of our desire?'

The Virgin started from her seat, & with a shriek
Fled back unhinder'd till she came into the vales of
    Har.

The End

THE MARRIAGE OF HEAVEN AND HELL

(About 1793)

THE ARGUMENT

Rintrah roars & shakes his fires in the burden'd air;
Hungry clouds swag on the deep.

Once meek, and in a perilous path,
The just man kept his course along
The vale of death.
Roses are planted where thorns grow,
And on the barren heath
Sing the honey bees.

Then the perilous path was planted,
And a river and a spring
On every cliff and tomb,
And on the bleached bones
Red clay brought forth;

Till the villain left the paths of ease,
To walk in perilous paths, and drive
The just man into barren climes.

Now the sneaking serpent walks
In mild humility,
And the just man rages in the wilds
Where lions roam.

Rintrah roars & shakes his fires in the burden'd air;
Hungry clouds swag on the deep.

As a new heaven is begun, and it is now thirty-three years since its advent, the Eternal Hell revives. And lo! Swedenborg is the Angel sitting at the tomb: his writings are the linen clothes folded up. Now is the dominion of Edom, & the return of Adam into Paradise: see Isaiah xxxiv & xxxv Chap.

Without Contraries is no progression. Attraction and Repulsion, Reason and Energy, Love and Hate, are necessary to Human existence.

From these contraries spring what the religious call Good & Evil. Good is the passive that obeys Reason. Evil is the active springing from Energy.

Good is Heaven. Evil is Hell.

THE VOICE OF THE DEVIL

All Bibles or sacred codes have been the causes of the following Errors.

1. That Man has two real existing principles, Viz: a Body & a Soul.

2. That Energy, call'd Evil, is alone from the Body, & that Reason, call'd Good, is alone from the Soul.

3. That God will torment Man in Eternity for following his Energies.

But the following Contraries to these are True.

1. Man has no Body distinct from his Soul; for that call'd Body is a portion of Soul discern'd by the five Senses, the chief inlets of Soul in this age.

2. Energy is the only life and is from the Body, and Reason is the bound or outward circumference of Energy.

3. Energy is Eternal Delight.

Those who restrain desire, do so because theirs is weak enough to be restrained; and the restrainer or reason usurps its place & governs the unwilling.

And being restrain'd, it by degrees becomes passive, till it is only the shadow of desire.

The history of this is written in Paradise Lost, & the Governor or Reason is call'd Messiah.

And the original Archangel, or possessor of the command of the heavenly host, is call'd the Devil or Satan, and his children are call'd Sin & Death.

But in the Book of Job, Milton's Messiah is call'd Satan.

For this history has been adopted by both parties.

It indeed appear'd to Reason as if Desire was cast out; but the Devil's account is, that the Messiah fell, & formed a heaven of what he stole from the Abyss.

This is shewn in the Gospel, where he prays to the Father to send the comforter, or Desire, that Reason may have Ideas to build on, the Jehovah of the Bible being no other than he who dwells in flaming fire.

Know that after Christ's death, he became Jehovah.

But in Milton, the Father is Destiny, the Son a Ratio of the five senses, & the Holy-ghost Vacuum!

Note. The reason Milton wrote in fetters when he wrote of Angels & God, and at liberty when of Devils & Hell, is because he was a true Poet and of the Devil's party without knowing it.

A MEMORABLE FANCY

As I was walking among the fires of hell, delighted with the enjoyments of Genius, which to Angels look like torment and insanity, I collected some of their Proverbs, thinking that as the sayings used in a nation mark its character, so the Proverbs of Hell shew the nature of Infernal wisdom better than any description of buildings or garments.

When I came home, on the abyss of the five senses, where a flat sided steep frowns over the present world, I saw a mighty Devil folded in black clouds hovering on the sides of the rock: with corroding fires he wrote the following sentence now percieved by the minds of men, & read by them on earth.

How do you know but ev'ry Bird that cuts the airy
    way,
Is an immense world of delight, clos'd by your senses
    five?

PROVERBS OF HELL

1. In seed time learn, in harvest teach, in winter enjoy.
2. Drive your cart and your plow over the bones of the dead.
3. The road of excess leads to the palace of wisdom.
4. Prudence is a rich ugly old maid courted by Incapacity.
5. He who desires but acts not, breeds pestilence.
6. The cut worm forgives the plow.
7. Dip him in the river who loves water.
8. A fool sees not the same tree that a wise man sees.
9. He whose face gives no light, shall never become a star.
10. Eternity is in love with the productions of time.
11. The busy bee has no time for sorrow.
12. The hours of folly are measur'd by the clock, but of wisdom no clock can measure.
13. All wholsom food is caught without a net or a trap.
14. Bring out number weight & measure in a year of dearth.
15. No bird soars too high if he soars with his own wings.
16. A dead body revenges not injuries.
17. The most sublime act is to set another before you.
18. If the fool would persist in his folly he would become wise.

19. Folly is the cloke of knavery.
20. Shame is Pride's cloke.
21. Prisons are built with stones of Law, Brothels with bricks of Religion.
22. The pride of the peacock is the glory of God.
23. The lust of the goat is the bounty of God.
24. The wrath of the lion is the wisdom of God.
25. The nakedness of woman is the work of God.
26. Excess of sorrow laughs. Excess of joy weeps.
27. The roaring of lions, the howling of wolves, the raging of the stormy sea, and the destructive sword, are portions of eternity too great for the eye of man.
28. The fox condemns the trap, not himself.
29. Joys impregnate. Sorrows bring forth.
30. Let man wear the fell of the lion, woman the fleece of the sheep.
31. The bird a nest, the spider a web, man friendship.
32. The selfish smiling fool, & the sullen frowning fool shall be both thought wise, that they may be a rod.
33. What is now proved was once only imagin'd.
34. The rat, the mouse, the fox, the rabbet, watch the roots; the lion, the tyger, the horse, the elephant, watch the fruits.
35. The cistern contains: the fountain overflows.
36. One thought fills immensity.
37. Always be ready to speak your mind and a base man will avoid you.

38. Every thing possible to be believ'd is an image of truth.
39. The eagle never lost so much time as when he submitted to learn of the crow.
40. The fox provides for himself, but God provides for the lion.
41. Think in the morning. Act in the noon. Eat in the evening. Sleep in the night.
42. He who has suffer'd you to impose on him knows you.
43. As the plow follows words, so God rewards prayers.
44. The tygers of wrath are wiser than the horses of instruction.
45. Expect poison from the standing water.
46. You never know what is enough unless you know what is more than enough.
47. Listen to the fool's reproach! it is a kingly title!
48. The eyes of fire, the nostrils of air, the mouth of water, the beard of earth.
49. The weak in courage is strong in cunning.
50. The apple tree never asks the beech how he shall grow, nor the lion the horse, how he shall take his prey.
51. The thankful reciever bears a plentiful harvest.
52. If others had not been foolish, we should be so.
53. The soul of sweet delight can never be defil'd.

54. When thou seest an Eagle, thou seest a portion of Genius. lift up thy head!
55. As the catterpiller chooses the fairest leaves to lay her eggs on, so the priest lays his curse on the fairest joys.
56. To create a little flower is the labour of ages.
57. Damn braces. Bless relaxes.
58. The best wine is the oldest, the best water the newest.
59. Prayers plow not! Praises reap not!
60. Joys laugh not! Sorrows weep not!
61. The head Sublime, the heart Pathos, the genitals Beauty, the hands & feet Proportion.
62. As the air to a bird or the sea to a fish, so is contempt to the contemptible.
63. The crow wish'd every thing was black, the owl that every thing was white.
64. Exuberance is Beauty.
65. If the lion was advised by the fox, he would be cunning.
66. Improvement makes strait roads, but the crooked roads without Improvement are roads of Genius.
67. Sooner murder an infant in its cradle than nurse unacted desires.
68. Where man is not, nature is barren.
69. Truth can never be told so as to be understood, and not be believ'd.
70. Enough! or Too much.

The ancient Poets animated all sensible objects with Gods or Geniuses, calling them by the names and adorning them with the properties of woods, rivers, mountains, lakes, cities, nations, and whatever their enlarged & numerous senses could percieve.

And particularly they studied the genius of each city & country, placing it under its mental deity;

Till a system was formed, which some took advantage of & enslav'd the vulgar by attempting to realize or abstract the mental deities from their objects: thus began Priesthood,

Choosing forms of worship from poetic tales.

And at length they pronounc'd that the Gods had order'd such things.

Thus men forgot that All deities reside in the human breast.

A MEMORABLE FANCY

The Prophets Isaiah and Ezekiel dined with me, and I asked them how they dared so roundly to assert that God spoke to them; and whether they did not think at the time that they would be misunderstood, & so be the cause of imposition.

Isaiah answer'd: 'I saw no God, nor heard any, in a finite organical perception; but my senses discover'd the infinite in every thing, and as I was then perswaded, & remain confirm'd, that the voice of honest indignation is the voice of God, I cared not for consequences, but wrote.'

Then I asked: 'does a firm perswasion that a thing is so, make it so?'

He replied: 'All poets believe that it does, & in ages of imagination this firm perswasion removed mountains; but many are not capable of a firm perswasion of any thing.'

Then Ezekiel said: 'The philosophy of the east taught the first principles of human perception: some nations held one principle for the origin & some another: we of Israel taught that the Poetic Genius (as you now call it) was the first principle, and all the others merely derivative, which was the cause of our despising the Priests & Philosophers of other countries, and prophecying that all Gods would at last be proved to originate in ours & to be the tributaries of the Poetic Genius: it was this that our great poet, King David, desired so fervently & invokes so patheticly, saying by this he conquers enemies & governs kingdoms; and we so loved our God, that we cursed in his name all the deities of surrounding nations, and asserted that they had rebelled: from these opinions the vulgar came to think that all nations would at last be subject to the jews.'

'This,' said he, 'like all firm perswasions, is come to pass; for all nations believe the jews' code and worship the jews' god, and what greater subjection can be?'

I heard this with some wonder, & must confess my own conviction. After dinner I ask'd Isaiah to favour the world with his lost works; he said none of equal value was lost. Ezekiel said the same of his.

I also asked Isaiah what made him go naked and barefoot three years? he answer'd, 'the same that made our friend Diogenes the Grecian.'

I then asked Ezekiel why he eat dung & lay so long on his right & left side? he answer'd, 'the desire of raising other men into a perception of the infinite: this the North American tribes practise, & is he honest who resists his genius or conscience only for the sake of present ease or gratification?'

The ancient tradition that the world will be consumed in fire at the end of six thousand years is true, as I have heard from Hell;

For the cherub with his flaming sword is hereby commanded to leave his guard at tree of life, and when he does, the whole creation will be consumed and appear infinite and holy, whereas it now appears finite & corrupt.

This will come to pass by an improvement of sensual enjoyment.

But first the notion that man has a body distinct from his soul is to be expunged: this I shall do, by printing in the infernal method, by corrosives, which in Hell are salutary and medicinal, melting apparent surfaces away, and displaying the infinite which was hid.

If the doors of perception were cleansed, every thing would appear to man as it is, infinite.

For man has closed himself up, till he sees all things thro' narrow chinks of his cavern.

A MEMORABLE FANCY

I was in a Printing house in Hell & saw the method in which knowledge is transmitted from generation to generation.

In the first chamber was a Dragon-Man, clearing away the rubbish from a cave's mouth: within, a number of Dragons were hollowing the cave.

In the second chamber was a Viper folding round the rock & the cave, and others adorning it with gold silver and precious stones.

In the third chamber was an Eagle with wings and feathers of air: he caused the inside of the cave to be infinite: around were numbers of Eagle like men, who built palaces in the immense cliffs.

In the fourth chamber were Lions of flaming fire, raging around & melting the metals into living fluids.

In the fifth chamber were Unnam'd forms, which cast the metals into the expanse.

There they were reciev'd by Men who occupied the sixth chamber, and took the forms of books & were arranged in libraries.

The Giants who formed this world into its sensual existence and now seem to live in it in chains, are in truth the causes of its life & the sources of all activity; but the chains are the cunning of weak and tame minds which have power to resist energy: according to the proverb, the weak in courage is strong in cunning.

Thus one portion of being is the Prolific; the other, the Devouring: to the devourer it seems as if the producer was in his chains; but it is not so, he only takes portions of existence and fancies that the whole.

But the Prolific would cease to be Prolific unless the Devourer as a sea recieved the excess of his delights.

Some will say, 'Is not God alone the Prolific?' I answer, 'God only Acts and Is, in existing beings or Men.'

These two classes of men are always upon earth, & they should be enemies: whoever tries to reconcile them seeks to destroy existence.

Religion is an endeavour to reconcile the two.

Note. Jesus Christ did not wish to unite, but to separate them, as in the Parable of sheep and goats! & he says, 'I came not to send Peace but a Sword.'

Messiah or Satan or Tempter was formerly thought to be one of the Antediluvians who are our Energies.

A MEMORABLE FANCY

An Angel came to me and said: 'O pitiable foolish young man! O horrible! O dreadful state! consider the hot burning dungeon thou art preparing for thyself to all eternity, to which thou art going in such career.'

I said, 'perhaps you will be willing to shew me my eternal lot & we will contemplate together upon it, and see whether your lot or mine is most desirable.'

So he took me thro' a stable & thro' a church & down into the church vault, at the end of which was a mill: thro' the mill we went, and came to a cave: down the winding cavern we groped our tedious way till a void boundless as a nether sky appear'd beneath us, & we held by the roots of trees and hung over this immensity; but I said, 'if you please we will commit ourselves to this void, and see whether providence is here also: if you will not, I will?' but he answer'd, 'do not presume, O young man, but as we here remain, behold thy lot which will soon appear when the darkness passes away.'

So I remain'd with him, sitting in the twisted root of an oak: he was suspended in a fungus, which hung with the head downward into the deep.

By degrees we beheld the infinite Abyss, fiery as the smoke of a burning city; beneath us at an immense distance was the sun, black but shining: round it were fiery tracks on which revolv'd vast spiders crawling after their prey, which flew, or rather swum in the infinite deep, in the most terrific shapes of animals sprung from corruption; & the air was full of them & seem'd composed of them: these are Devils, and are called Powers of the air. I now asked my companion which was my eternal lot? he said, 'between the black & white spiders.'

But now, from between the black & white spiders, a cloud and fire burst and rolled thro' the deep, blackning all beneath, so that the nether deep grew black as a sea & rolled with a terrible noise: beneath us was nothing now to be seen but a black tempest, till looking east between the clouds & the waves, we saw a cataract of blood mixed with fire, and not many stone's throw from us appear'd and sunk again the scaly fold of a monstrous serpent: at last, to the east, distant about three degrees, appear'd a fiery crest above the waves: slowly it reared like a ridge of golden rocks till we discover'd two globes of crimson fire, from which the sea fled away in clouds of smoke; and now we saw it was the head of Leviathan; his forehead was divided into streaks of green & purple like those on a tyger's forehead: soon we saw his mouth & red gills hang just above the raging foam, tinging the black deep with beams of blood, advancing toward us with all the fury of a spiritual existence.

195

My friend the Angel climb'd up from his station into the mill; I remain'd alone, & then this appearance was no more, but I found myself sitting on a pleasant bank beside a river by moonlight, hearing a harper who sung to the harp, & his theme was: 'The man who never alters his opinion is like standing water, & breeds reptiles of the mind.'

But I arose and sought for the mill & there I found my Angel, who surprised asked me how I escaped?

I answer'd: 'All that we saw was owing to your metaphysics; for when you ran away, I found myself on a bank by moonlight hearing a harper. But now we have seen my eternal lot, shall I shew you yours?' he laugh'd at my proposal; but I by force suddenly caught him in my arms, & flew westerly thro' the night, till we were elevated above the earth's shadow; then I flung myself with him directly into the body of the sun: here I clothed myself in white, & taking in my hand Swedenborg's volumes, sunk from the glorious clime, and passed all the planets till we came to saturn: here I staid to rest, & then leap'd into the void between saturn and the fixed stars.

'Here,' said I, 'is your lot, in this space, if space it may be call'd.' Soon we saw the stable and the church, & I took him to the altar and open'd the Bible, and lo! it was a deep pit, into which I descended driving the Angel before me: soon we saw seven houses of brick:

one we enter'd; in it were a number of monkeys, baboons, & all of that species, chain'd by the middle, grinning and snatching at one another, but withheld by the shortness of their chains: however, I saw that they sometimes grew numerous, and then the weak were caught by the strong, and with a grinning aspect, first coupled with & then devour'd, by plucking off first one limb and then another, till the body was left a helpless trunk: this, after grinning & kissing it with seeming fondness, they devour'd too; and here & there I saw one savourily picking the flesh off of his own tail: as the stench terribly annoy'd us both, we went into the mill, & I in my hand brought the skeleton of a body, which in the mill was Aristotle's Analytics.

So the Angel said: 'thy phantasy has imposed upon me & thou oughtest to be ashamed.'

I answer'd: 'we impose on one another, & it is but lost time to converse with you whose works are only Analytics.'

I have always found that Angels have the vanity to speak of themselves as the only wise: this they do with a confident insolence sprouting from systematic reasoning.

Thus Swedenborg boasts that what he writes is new, tho' it is only the Contents or Index of already publish'd books.

A man carried a monkey about for a shew, & because he was a little wiser than the monkey, grew vain, and conciev'd himself as much wiser than seven men. It is so with Swedenborg: he shews the folly of churches & exposes hypocrites, till he imagines that all are religious, & himself the single one on earth that ever broke a net.

Now hear a plain fact: Swedenborg has not written one new truth. Now hear another: he has written all the old falshoods.

And now hear the reason. He conversed with Angels who are all religious, & conversed not with Devils who all hate religion, for he was incapable thro' his conceited notions.

Thus Swedenborg's writings are a recapitulation of all superficial opinions, and an analysis of the more sublime, but no further.

Have now another plain fact. Any man of mechanical talents may, from the writings of Paracelsus or Jacob Behmen, produce ten thousand volumes of equal value with Swedenborg's, and from those of Dante or Shakespear an infinite number.

But when he has done this, let him not say that he knows better than his master, for he only holds a candle in sunshine.

A MEMORABLE FANCY

Once I saw a Devil in a flame of fire, who arose before an Angel that sat on a cloud, and the Devil utter'd these words:

'The worship of God is, Honouring his gifts in other men, each according to his genius, and loving the greatest men best: those who envy or calumniate great men hate God, for there is no other God.'

The Angel hearing this became almost blue; but mastering himself he grew yellow, & at last white pink & smiling, and then replied:

'Thou Idolater: is not God One? & is not he visible in Jesus Christ? and has not Jesus Christ given his sanction to the law of ten commandments? and are not all other men fools, sinners, & nothings?'

The Devil answer'd: 'bray a fool in a morter with wheat, yet shall not his folly be beaten out of him: if Jesus Christ is the greatest man, you ought to love him in the greatest degree: now hear how he has given his sanction to the law of ten commandments: did he not mock at the sabbath, and so mock the sabbath's God? murder those who were murder'd because of him? turn away the law from the woman taken in adultery? steal the labor of others to support him? bear false witness when he omitted making a defence before Pilate? covet when he pray'd for his disciples, and when he bid them shake off the dust of their feet against such as refused to lodge them? I tell you, no virtue can exist without breaking these ten commandments. Jesus was all virtue, and acted from impulse, not from rules.'

When he had so spoken, I beheld the Angel, who stretched out his arms embracing the flames of fire, & he was consumed and arose as Elijah.

Note. This Angel, who is now become a Devil, is my particular friend: we often read the Bible together in its infernal or diabolical sense, which the world shall have if they behave well.

I have also, The Bible of Hell, which the world shall have whether they will or no.

One Law for the Lion & Ox is Oppression.

A SONG OF LIBERTY

1. The Eternal Female groan'd! it was heard over all the Earth.

2. Albion's coast is sick silent: the American meadows faint!

3. Shadows of Prophecy shiver along by the lakes and the rivers and mutter across the ocean: 'France, rend down thy dungeon.

4. 'Golden Spain, burst the barriers of old Rome.

5. 'Cast thy keys, O Rome, into the deep down falling, even to eternity down falling,

6. 'And weep.'

7. In her trembling hands she took the new born terror howling.

8. On those infinite mountains of light, now barr'd out by the atlantic sea, the new born fire stood before the starry king!

9. Flag'd with grey brow'd snows and thunderous visages, the jealous wings wav'd over the deep.

10. The speary hand burned aloft, unbuckled was the shield; forth went the hand of jealousy among the flaming hair, and hurl'd the new born wonder thro' the starry night.

11. The fire, the fire, is falling!

12. Look up! look up! O citizen of London, enlarge thy countenance. O Jew, leave counting gold! return to thy

oil and wine. O African! black African! (go, winged thought, widen his forehead.)

13. The fiery limbs, the flaming hair, shot like the sinking sun into the western sea.

14. Wak'd from his eternal sleep, the hoary element roaring fled away.

15. Down rush'd, beating his wings in vain, the jealous king; his grey brow'd councellors, thunderous warriors, curl'd veterans, among helms, and shields, and chariots, horses, elephants, banners, castles, slings and rocks.

16. Falling, rushing, ruining! buried in the ruins, on Urthona's dens.

17. All night beneath the ruins, then their sullen flames faded emerge round the gloomy king.

18. With thunder and fire, leading his starry hosts thro' the waste wilderness, he promulgates his ten commands, glancing his beamy eyelids over the deep in dark dismay,

19. Where the son of fire in his eastern cloud, while the morning plumes her golden breast,

20. Spurning the clouds written with curses, stamps the stony law to dust, loosing the eternal horses from the dens of night, crying, 'Empire is no more! and now the lion & wolf shall cease.'

CHORUS

Let the Priests of the Raven of dawn, no longer, in deadly black, with hoarse note, curse the sons of joy. Nor his accepted brethren, whom, tyrant, he calls free, lay the bound or build the roof. Nor pale religious letchery call that Virginity that wishes but acts not! For every thing that lives is Holy.

THE FIRST BOOK OF URIZEN

(1794)

PRELUDIUM TO THE BOOK OF URIZEN

Of the primeval Priest's assum'd power
When Eternals spurn'd back his religion
And gave him a place in the north,
Obscure, shadowy, void, solitary.

Eternals, I hear your call gladly.
Dictate swift winged words, & fear not
To unfold your dark visions of torment

Chap: I

1. Lo, a shadow of horror is risen
   In Eternity! Unknown, unprolific,
   Self-clos'd, all-repelling: what Demon
   Hath form'd this abominable void,
   This soul-shudd'ring vacuum? Some said
   'It is Urizen.' But unknown, abstracted,
   Brooding secret, the dark power hid.

2. Times on times he divided, & measur'd
   Space by space in his ninefold darkness,
   Unseen, unknown: changes appear'd
   Like desolate mountains rifted furious
   By the black winds of perturbation.

3. For he strove in battles dire,
   In unseen conflictions with shapes
   Bred from his forsaken wilderness
   Of beast, bird, fish, serpent & element,
   Combustion, blast, vapour and cloud.

4. Dark revolving in silent activity,
   Unseen in tormenting passions,
   An activity unknown and horrible,
   A self-contemplating shadow
   In enormous labours occupied.

5. But Eternals beheld his vast forests.
   Age on ages he lay, clos'd, unknown,
   Brooding, shut in the deep; all avoid
   The petrific abominable chaos.

6. His cold horrors silent, dark Urizen
   Prepar'd; his ten thousands of thunders
   Rang'd in gloom'd array, stretch out across
   The dread world; & the rolling of wheels
   As of swelling seas, sound in his clouds,
   In his hills of stor'd snows, in his mountains
   Of hail & ice: voices of terror
   Are heard like thunders of autumn
   When the cloud blazes over the harvests.

Chap: II

1. Earth was not, nor globes of attraction.
   The will of the Immortal expanded
   Or contracted his all flexible senses.
   Death was not, but eternal life sprung.

2. The sound of a trumpet the heavens
   Awoke, & vast clouds of blood roll'd
   Round the dim rocks of Urizen, so nam'd
   That solitary one in Immensity.

3. Shrill the trumpet: & myriads of Eternity
   Muster around the bleak desarts
   Now fill'd with clouds, darkness & waters
   That roll'd perplex'd lab'ring, & utter'd
   Words articulate bursting in thunders
   That roll'd on the tops of his mountains

4. From the depths of dark solitude: 'From
   The eternal abode, in my holiness
   Hidden, set apart in my stern counsels
   Reserv'd for the days of futurity,
   I have sought for a joy without pain,
   For a solid without fluctuation.
   Why will you die, O Eternals?
   Why live in unquenchable burnings?

5. 'First I fought with the fire, consum'd
   Inwards into a deep world within,
   A void immense, wild, dark & deep,
   Where nothing was, Nature's wide womb:
   And self-balanc'd, stretch'd o'er the void,
   I alone, even I! the winds merciless
   Bound; but condensing in torrents
   They fall and fall; strong I repell'd
   The vast waves, & arose on the waters
   A wide world of solid obstruction.

6. 'Here alone I, in books form'd of metals,
   Have written the secrets of wisdom,
   The secrets of dark contemplation,
   By fightings and conflicts dire
   With terrible monsters Sin-bred
   Which the bosoms of all inhabit,
   Seven deadly Sins of the soul.

7. 'Lo! I unfold my darkness, and on
This rock place with strong hand the Book
Of eternal brass, written in my solitude:

8. 'Laws of peace, of love, of unity,
Of pity, compassion, forgiveness.
Let each chuse one habitation,
His ancient infinite mansion,
One command, one joy, one desire,
One curse, one weight, one measure,
One King, one God, one Law.'

Chap: III

1. The voice ended: they saw his pale visage
Emerge from the darkness, his hand
On the rock of eternity unclasping
The Book of brass. Rage siez'd the strong,

2. Rage, fury, intense indignation.
In cataracts of fire, blood & gall,
In whirlwinds of sulphurous smoke
And enormous forms of energy,
All the seven deadly sins of the soul
In living creations appear'd
In the flames of eternal fury.

3. Sund'ring, dark'ning, thund'ring!
   Rent away with a terrible crash,
   Eternity roll'd wide apart,
   Wide asunder rolling
   Mountainous, all around
   Departing, departing, departing,
   Leaving ruinous fragments of life
   Hanging, frowning cliffs, & all between
   An ocean of voidness unfathomable.

4. The roaring fires ran o'er the heav'ns
   In whirlwinds & cataracts of blood,
   And o'er the dark desarts of Urizen
   Fires pour thro' the void on all sides
   On Urizen's self-begotten armies.

5. But no light from the fires, all was darkness
   In the flames of Eternal fury.

6. In fierce anguish & quenchless flames
   To the desarts and rocks he ran raging
   To hide, but he could not: combining,
   He dug mountains & hills in vast strength,
   He piled them in incessant labour,
   In howlings & pangs & fierce madness,
   Long periods in burning fires labouring,
   Till hoary and age-broke and aged,
   In despair and the shadows of death.

7. And a roof vast, petrific, around
   On all sides he fram'd, like a womb,
   Where thousands of rivers in veins
   Of blood pour down the mountains to cool
   The eternal fires beating without
   From Eternals; & like a black globe
   View'd by sons of Eternity, standing
   On the shore of the infinite ocean,
   Like a human heart strugling & beating
   The vast world of Urizen appear'd.

8. And Los round the dark globe of Urizen
   Kept watch for Eternals to confine
   The obscure separation alone;
   For Eternity stood wide apart
   As the stars are apart from the earth.

9. Los wept howling around the dark Demon,
   And cursing his lot; for in anguish
   Urizen was rent from his side,
   And a fathomless void for his feet,
   And intense fires for his dwelling.

10. But Urizen laid in a stony sleep,
    Unorganiz'd, rent from Eternity.

11. The Eternals said, 'What is this? Death.
    Urizen is a clod of clay.'

12. Los howl'd in a dismal stupor,
    Groaning! gnashing! groaning!
    Till the wrenching apart was healed.

13. But the wrenching of Urizen heal'd not.
    Cold, featureless, flesh or clay
    Rifted with direful changes,
    He lay in a dreamless night,

14. Till Los rouz'd his fires, affrighted
    At the formless unmeasurable death.

Chap: IV

1. Los, smitten with astonishment,
   Frighten'd at the hurtling bones

2. And at the surging sulphureous
   Perturbed Immortal, mad raging

3. In whirlwinds & pitch & nitre
   Round the furious limbs of Los.

4. And Los formed nets & gins
   And threw the nets round about.

5. He watch'd in shudd'ring fear
   The dark changes, & bound every change
   With rivets of iron & brass.

6. And these were the changes of Urizen:

Chap: IV [a]

1. Ages on ages roll'd over him,
   In stony sleep ages roll'd over him,
   Like a dark waste stretching chang'able
   By earthquakes riv'n, belching sullen fires:
   On ages roll'd ages in ghastly
   Sick torment; around him in whirlwinds
   Of darkness the eternal Prophet howl'd,
   Beating still on his rivets of iron,
   Pouring sodor of iron, dividing
   The horrible night into watches.

2. And Urizen (so his eternal name)
   His prolific delight obscur'd more & more
   In dark secresy, hiding in surgeing
   Sulphureous fluid his phantasies.
   The Eternal Prophet heav'd the dark bellows
   And turn'd restless the tongs, and the hammer
   Incessant beat, forging chains new & new,
   Numb'ring with links hours, days & years.

3. The Eternal mind bounded began to roll
   Eddies of wrath ceaseless round & round,
   And the sulphureous foam, surging thick,
   Settled, a lake bright & shining clear,
   White as the snow on the mountains cold.

4. Forgetfulness, dumbness, necessity!
   In chains of the mind locked up,
   Like fetters of ice shrinking together,
   Disorganiz'd, rent from Eternity.
   Los beat on his fetters of iron,
   And heated his furnaces & pour'd
   Iron sodor and sodor of brass.

5. Restless turn'd the immortal inchain'd,
   Heaving dolorous! anguish'd unbearable,
   Till a roof, shaggy wild, inclos'd
   In an orb his fountain of thought.

6. In a horrible dreamful slumber,
   Like the linked infernal chain
   A vast Spine writh'd in torment
   Upon the winds, shooting pain'd
   Ribs, like a bending cavern;
   And bones of solidness froze
   Over all his nerves of joy.
   And a first Age passed over,
   And a state of dismal woe.

7. From the caverns of his jointed Spine
   Down sunk with fright a red
   Round globe, hot burning, deep
   Deep down into the Abyss,
   Panting, Conglobing, Trembling,
   Shooting out ten thousand branches
   Around his solid bones.
   And a second Age passed over,
   And a state of dismal woe.

8. In harrowing fear rolling round,
   His nervous brain shot branches
   Round the branches of his heart
   On high into two little orbs,
   And fixed in two little caves
   Hiding carefully from the wind,
   His Eyes beheld the deep.
   And a third Age passed over,
   And a state of dismal woe.

9. The pangs of hope began.
   In heavy pain, striving, struggling,
   Two Ears in close volutions
   From beneath his orbs of vision
   Shot spiring out and petrified
   As they grew. And a fourth Age passed,
   And a state of dismal woe.

10. In ghastly torment sick,
    Hanging upon the wind,
    Two Nostrils bent down to the deep.
    And a fifth Age passed over,
    And a state of dismal woe.

11. In ghastly torment sick,
    Within his ribs bloated round
    A craving Hungry Cavern.
    Thence arose his channel'd Throat,
    And like a red flame, a Tongue
    Of thirst & of hunger appear'd.
    And a sixth Age passed over,
    And a state of dismal woe.

12. Enraged & stifled with torment,
    He threw his right Arm to the north,
    His left Arm to the south
    Shooting out in anguish deep,
    And his Feet stamp'd the nether Abyss
    In trembling & howling & dismay.
    And a seventh Age passed over,
    And a state of dismal woe.

Chap: V

1. In terrors Los shrunk from his task:
   His great hammer fell from his hand.
   His fires beheld, and sickening
   Hid their strong limbs in smoke;
   For with noises ruinous loud,
   With hurtlings & clashings & groans,
   The Immortal endur'd his chains,
   Tho' bound in a deadly sleep.

2. All the myriads of Eternity,
   All the wisdom & joy of life
   Roll like a sea around him,
   Except what his little orbs
   Of sight by degrees unfold.

3. And now his eternal life
   Like a dream was obliterated.

4. Shudd'ring, the Eternal Prophet smote
   With a stroke from his north to south region.
   The bellows & hammer are silent now,
   A nerveless silence his prophetic voice
   Siez'd; a cold solitude & dark void
   The Eternal Prophet & Urizen clos'd.

5. Ages on ages roll'd over them,
   Cut off from life & light, frozen
   Into horrible forms of deformity.
   Los suffer'd his fires to decay;
   Then he look'd back with anxious desire,
   But the space, undivided by existence,
   Struck horror into his soul.

6. Los wept, obscur'd with mourning,
   His bosom earthquak'd with sighs;
   He saw Urizen deadly black,
   In his chains bound, & Pity began.

7. In anguish dividing & dividing,
   For pity divides the soul.
   In pangs, eternity on eternity,
   Life in cataracts pour'd down his cliffs.
   The void shrunk the lymph into Nerves
   Wand'ring wide on the bosom of night,
   And left a round globe of blood
   Trembling upon the void.

Thus the Eternal Prophet was divided
Before the death image of Urizen;
For in changeable clouds and darkness,
In a winterly night beneath,
The Abyss of Los stretch'd immense,
And now seen, now obscur'd, to the eyes
Of Eternals the visions remote
Of the dark seperation appear'd.
As glasses discover Worlds
In the endless Abyss of space,
So the expanding eyes of Immortals
Beheld the dark visions of Los
And the globe of life blood trembling.

8. The globe of life blood trembled
Branching out into roots
Fibrous, writhing upon the winds,
Fibres of blood, milk and tears,
In pangs, eternity on eternity.
At length, in tears & cries imbodied,
A female form trembling and pale
Waves before his deathy face.

9. All Eternity shudder'd at sight
Of the first female now separate,
Pale as a cloud of snow
Waving before the face of Los.

10. Wonder, awe, fear, astonishment
    Petrify the eternal myriads
    At the first female form now separate.
    They call'd her Pity, and fled.

11. 'Spread a Tent with strong curtains around them.
    Let cords & stakes bind in the Void,
    That Eternals may no more behold them.'

12. They began to weave curtains of darkness,
    They erected large pillars round the Void,
    With golden hooks fasten'd in the pillars;
    With infinite labour the Eternals
    A woof wove, and called it Science.

Chap: VI

1. But Los saw the Female & pitied;
   He embrac'd her; she wept, she refus'd;
   In perverse and cruel delight
   She fled from his arms, yet he follow'd.

2. Eternity shudder'd when they saw
   Man begetting his likeness
   On his own divided image.

3. A time passed over: the Eternals
    Began to erect the tent,
    When Enitharmon sick
    Felt a Worm within her womb.

4. Yet helpless it lay like a Worm
    In the trembling womb
    To be moulded into existence.

5. All day the worm lay on her bosom;
    All night within her womb
    The worm lay, till it grew to a serpent
    With dolorous hissings & poisons
    Round Enitharmon's loins folding.

6. Coil'd within Enitharmon's womb
    The serpent grew, casting its scales;
    With sharp pangs the hissings began
    To change to a grating cry.
    Many sorrows and dismal throes,
    Many forms of fish, bird & beast
    Brought forth an Infant form
    Where was a worm before.

7. The Eternals their tent finished
   Alarm'd with these gloomy visions,
   When Enitharmon groaning
   Produc'd a man Child to the light.

8. A shriek ran thro' Eternity
   And a paralytic stroke
   At the birth of the Human shadow.

9. Delving earth in his resistless way,
   Howling, the Child with fierce flames
   Issu'd from Enitharmon.

10. The Eternals closed the tent;
    They beat down the stakes, the cords
    Stretch'd for a work of eternity.
    No more Los beheld Eternity.

11. In his hands he siez'd the infant;
    He bathed him in springs of sorrow;
    He gave him to Enitharmon.

Chap: VII

1. They named the child Orc; he grew,
   Fed with milk of Enitharmon.

2. Los awoke her. O sorrow & pain!
   A tight'ning girdle grew
   Around his bosom. In sobbings
   He burst the girdle in twain,
   But still another girdle
   Oppress'd his bosom. In sobbings
   Again he burst it. Again
   Another girdle succeeds.
   The girdle was form'd by day,
   By night was burst in twain.

3. These falling down on the rock
   Into an iron Chain,
   In each other link by link lock'd.

4. They took Orc to the top of a mountain.
   O how Enitharmon wept!
   They chain'd his young limbs to the rock
   With the Chain of Jealousy
   Beneath Urizen's deathful shadow.

5. The dead heard the voice of the child
   And began to awake from sleep;
   All things heard the voice of the child
   And began to awake to life.

6. And Urizen, craving with hunger,
   Stung with the odours of Nature,
   Explor'd his dens around.

7. He form'd a line & a plummet
   To divide the Abyss beneath;
   He form'd a dividing rule.

8. He formed scales to weigh,
   He formed massy weights,
   He formed a brazen quadrant,
   He formed golden compasses,
   And began to explore the Abyss;
   And he planted a garden of fruits.

9. But Los encircled Enitharmon
   With fires of Prophecy
   From the sight of Urizen & Orc,

10. And she bore an enormous race.

Chap: VIII

1. Urizen explor'd his dens,
   Mountain, moor & wildernesss,
   With a globe of fire lighting his journey,
   A fearful journey, annoy'd
   By cruel enormities, forms
   Of life on his forsaken mountains.

2. And his world teem'd vast enormities,
   Fright'ning, faithless, fawning
   Portions of life, similitudes
   Of a foot or a hand or a head
   Or a heart or an eye; they swam, mischevous
   Dread terrors, delighting in blood.

3. Most Urizen sicken'd to see
   His eternal creations appear
   Sons & daughters of sorrow on mountains
   Weeping! wailing! first Thiriel appear'd,
   Astonish'd at his own existence,
   Like a man from a cloud born, & Utha
   From the waters emerging, laments.
   Grodna rent the deep earth, howling
   Amaz'd; his heavens immense cracks
   Like the ground parch'd with heat: then Fuzon
   Flam'd out, first begotten, last born.
   All his eternal sons in like manner,

His daughters from green herbs & cattle,
From monsters & worms of the pit.

4. He, in darkness clos'd, view'd all his race,
   And his soul sicken'd! he curs'd
   Both sons and daughters, for he saw
   That no flesh nor spirit could keep
   His iron laws one moment.

5. For he saw that life liv'd upon death:
   The Ox in the slaughter house moans,
   The Dog at the wintry door.
   And he wept & he called it Pity,
   And his tears flowed down on the winds.

6. Cold he wander'd on high, over their cities
   In weeping & pain & woe;
   And where-ever he wander'd in sorrows
   Upon the aged heavens
   A cold shadow follow'd behind him
   Like a spider's web, moist, cold & dim,
   Drawing out from his sorrowing soul,
   The dungeon-like heaven dividing,
   Where ever the footsteps of Urizen
   Walk'd over the cities in sorrow;

7. Till a Web, dark & cold, throughout all
   The tormented element stretch'd
   From the sorrows of Urizen's soul;
   And the Web is a Female in embrio:
   None could break the Web, no wings of fire,

8. So twisted the cords & so knotted
   The meshes, twisted like to the human brain.

9. And all call'd it The Net of Religion.

Chap: IX

1. Then the Inhabitants of those Cities
   Felt their Nerves change into Marrow,
   And hardening Bones began
   In swift diseases and torments,
   In throbbings & shootings & grindings
   Thro' all the coasts, till weaken'd
   The Senses inward rush'd shrinking
   Beneath the dark net of infection;

2. Till the shrunken eyes, clouded over,
   Discern'd not the woven hipocrisy,
   But the streaky slime in their heavens,
   Brought together by narrowing perceptions,
   Appear'd transparent air; for their eyes

Grew small like the eyes of a man,
And in reptile forms shrinking together,
Of seven feet stature they remain'd.

3. Six days they shrunk up from existence
   And on the seventh day they rested,
   And they bless'd the seventh day, in sick hope,
   And forgot their eternal life.

4. And their thirty cities divided
   In form of a human heart.
   No more could they rise at will
   In the infinite void, but bound down
   To earth by their narrowing perceptions,
   They lived a period of years,
   Then left a noisom body
   To the jaws of devouring darkness.

5. And their children wept, & built
   Tombs in the desolate places,
   And form'd laws of prudence and call'd them
   The eternal laws of God.

6. And the thirty cities remain'd
   Surrounded by salt floods, now call'd
   Africa: its name was then Egypt.

7. The remaining sons of Urizen
   Beheld their brethren shrink together
   Beneath the Net of Urizen.
   Perswasion was in vain,
   For the ears of the inhabitants
   Were wither'd & deafn'd & cold,
   And their eyes could not discern
   Their brethren of other cities.

8. So Fuzon call'd all together
   The remaining children of Urizen,
   And they left the pendulous earth:
   They called it Egypt, & left it.

9. And the salt ocean rolled englob'd.

        The End of the
        book of Urizen

THE SONG OF LOS

(1795)

AFRICA

I will sing you a song of Los, the Eternal Prophet:
He sung it to four harps at the tables of Eternity.
              In heart-formed Africa
Urizen faded! Ariston shudder'd!
        And thus the Song began:

Adam stood in the garden of Eden
And Noah on the mountains of Ararat;
They saw Urizen give his Laws to the Nations
By the hands of the children of Los.

Adam shudder'd! Noah faded! black grew the sunny
        African
When Rintrah gave Abstract Philosophy to Brama in
        the East.
        (Night spoke to the Cloud!
'Lo, these Human form'd spirits, in smiling hipocrisy
        War
Against one another; so let them War on, slaves to the
        eternal Elements.')
Noah shrunk beneath the waters;

Abram fled in fires from Chaldea;
Moses beheld upon Mount Sinai forms of dark
    delusion.

To Trismegistus Palamabron gave an abstract Law;
To Pythagoras, Socrates & Plato.

Times rolled on o'er all the sons of Har, time after
    time.
Orc on Mount Atlas howl'd, chain'd down with the
    Chain of Jealousy.
Then Oothoon hover'd over Judah & Jerusalem,
And Jesus heard her voice (a man of sorrows); he
    reciev'd
A Gospel from wretched Theotormon.
The human race began to wither, for the healthy built
Secluded places, fearing the joys of Love,
And the diseased only propagated.
So Antamon call'd up Leutha from her valleys of
    delight
And to Mahomet a loose Bible gave.

But in the North, to Odin Sotha gave a Code of War,
Because of Diralada, thinking to reclaim his joy.

These were the Churches, Hospitals, Castles, Palaces,
Like nets & gins & traps to catch the joys of Eternity,
        And all the rest a desart,
Till like a dream Eternity was obliterated & erased,

Since that dread day when Har and Heva fled
Because their brethren & sisters liv'd in War & Lust;
And as they fled, they shrunk
Into two narrow doleful forms
Creeping in reptile flesh upon
The bosom of the ground,
And all the vast of Nature shrunk
Before their shrunken eyes.

Thus the terrible race of Los & Enitharmon gave
Laws & Religions to the sons of Har, binding them
    more
And more to Earth: closing and restraining,
Till a Philosophy of Five Senses was complete.
Urizen wept & gave it into the hands of Newton &
    Locke.

Clouds roll heavy upon the Alps round Rousseau &
    Voltaire,
And on the mountains of Lebanon round the deceased
    Gods
Of Asia, & on the desarts of Africa round the Fallen
    Angels.
The Guardian Prince of Albion burns in his nightly
    tent.

ASIA

The Kings of Asia heard
The howl rise up from Europe!
And each ran out from his Web,
From his ancient woven Den;
For the darkness of Asia was startled
At the thick-flaming, thought-creating fires of Orc.

And the Kings of Asia stood
And cried in bitterness of soul:
   'Shall not the King call for Famine from the heath,
Nor the Priest for Pestilence from the fen?
To restrain! to dismay! to thin!
The inhabitants of mountain and plain
In the day of full-feeding prosperity
And the night of delicious songs.

'Shall not the Councellor throw his curb
Of Poverty on the laborious?
To fix the price of labour,
To invent allegoric riches,

'And the privy admonishers of men
Call for fires in the City,
For heaps of smoking ruins
In the night of prosperity & wantonness,

'To turn man from his path,
To restrain the child from the womb,
To cut off the bread from the city,
That the remnant may learn to obey,

'That the pride of the heart may fail,
That the lust of the eyes may be quench'd,
That the delicate ear in its infancy
May be dull'd, and the nostrils clos'd up,
To teach mortal worms the path
That leads from the gates of the Grave.'

      Urizen heard them cry,
And his shudd'ring waving wings
Went enormous above the red flames
Drawing clouds of despair thro' the heavens
Of Europe as he went.
And his Books of brass, iron & gold
Melted over the land as he flew
Heavy-waving, howling, weeping.

        And he stood over Judea,
        And stay'd in his ancient place,
        And stretch'd his clouds over Jerusalem;

        For Adam, a mouldering skeleton,
        Lay bleach'd on the garden of Eden,

And Noah, as white as snow,
On the mountains of Ararat.

Then the thunders of Urizen bellow'd aloud
From his woven darkness above.
Orc, raging in European darkness,
Arose like a pillar of fire above the Alps,
Like a serpent of fiery flame!

       The sullen Earth
        Shrunk!

Forth from the dead dust, rattling bones to bones
Join: shaking convuls'd, the shiv'ring clay breathes
And all flesh naked stands: Fathers and Friends,
Mothers & Infants, Kings & Warriors.

    The Grave shrieks with delight, & shakes
    Her hollow womb, & clasps the solid stem.
    Her bosom swells with wild desire,
    And milk & blood & glandous wine
    In rivers rush & shout & dance
    On mountain, dale and plain.

      The SONG of LOS is Ended
        Urizen Wept.

THE BOOK OF LOS

(1795)

Chap: I

1. *ENO, aged Mother*
   Who the chariot of Leutha guides
   Since the day of thunders in old time,

2. *Sitting beneath the eternal Oak,*
   Trembled and shook the steadfast Earth,
   And thus her speech broke forth:

3. *'O Times remote!*
   When Love & Joy were adoration
   And none impure were deem'd,
   Not Eyeless Covet,
   Nor Thin-lip'd Envy,
   Nor Bristled Wrath,
   Nor Curled Wantonness;

4. *'But Covet was poured full,*
   Envy fed with fat of lambs,
   Wrath with lion's gore,
   Wantonness lull'd to sleep
   With the virgin's lute
   Or sated with her love,

5. *'Till Covet broke his locks & bars*
   And slept with open doors,
   Envy sung at the rich man's feast,
   Wrath was follow'd up and down
   By a little ewe lamb,
   And Wantonness on his own true love
   Begot a giant race.'

6. Raging furious, the flames of desire
   Ran thro' heaven & earth, living flames,
   Intelligent, organiz'd, arm'd
   With destruction & plagues. In the midst
   The Eternal Prophet, bound in a chain,
   Compell'd to watch Urizen's shadow,

7. Rag'd with curses & sparkles of fury.
   Round the flames roll as Los hurls his chains,
   Mounting up from his fury, condens'd,
   Rolling round & round, mounting on high
   Into vacuum, into non-entity
   Where nothing was! dash'd wide apart,
   His feet stamp the eternal fierce-raging
   Rivers of wide flame; they roll round
   And round on all sides, making their way
   Into darkness and shadowy obscurity.

8. Wide apart stood the fires. Los remain'd
In the void between fire and fire.
In trembling and horror they beheld him;
They stood wide apart, driv'n by his hands
And his feet which the nether abyss
Stamp'd in fury and hot indignation.

9. But no light from the fires, all was
Darkness round Los; heat was not, for bound up
Into fiery spheres from his fury
The gigantic flames trembled and hid.

10. Coldness, darkness, obstruction, a Solid
Without fluctuation, hard as adamant,
Black as marble of Egypt impenetrable,
Bound in the fierce raging Immortal;
And the separated fires, froze in
A vast solid without fluctuation,
Bound in his expanding clear senses.

Chap: II

1. The Immortal stood frozen amidst
The vast rock of eternity times
And times, a night of vast durance,
Impatient, stifled, stiffen'd, hard'ned,

2. Till impatience no longer could bear
   The hard bondage, rent, rent the vast solid,
   With a crash from immense to immense

3. Crack'd across into numberless fragments.
   The Prophetic wrath, strugling for vent,
   Hurls apart, stamping furious to dust,
   And crumbling with bursting sobs, heaves
   The black marble on high into fragments.

4. Hurl'd apart on all sides as a falling
   Rock, the innumerable fragments away
   Fell asunder; and horrible vacuum
   Beneath him & on all sides round.

5. Falling falling! Los fell & fell,
   Sunk precipitant, heavy, down, down,
   Times on times, night on night, day on day:
   Truth has bounds, Error none: falling, falling;
   Years on years, and ages on ages
   Still he fell thro' the void, still a void
   Found for falling day & night without end;
   For tho' day or night was not, their spaces
   Were measur'd by his incessant whirls
   In the horrid vacuity bottomless.

6. The Immortal revolving, indignant
   First in wrath threw his limbs, like the babe
   New born into our world: wrath subsided
   And contemplative thoughts first arose.
   Then aloft his head rear'd in the Abyss
   And his downward-borne fall chang'd oblique.

7. Many ages of groans, till there grew
   Branchy forms organizing the Human
   Into finite inflexible organs,

8. Till in process from falling he bore
   Sidelong on the purple air, wafting
   The weak breeze in efforts o'erwearied.

9. Incessant the falling Mind labour'd
   Organizing itself, till the Vacuum
   Became element pliant to rise
   Or to fall, or to swim, or to fly,
   With ease searching the dire vacuity.

Chap: III

1. The Lungs heave incessant, dull and heavy,
   For as yet were all other parts formless,
   Shiv'ring, clinging around like a cloud,
   Dim & glutinous as the white Polypus
   Driv'n by waves & englob'd on the tide.

2. And the unformed part crav'd repose.
   Sleep began; the Lungs heave on the wave,
   Weary, overweigh'd, sinking beneath.
   In a stifling black fluid he woke:

3. He arose on the waters, but soon
   Heavy falling, his organs, like roots
   Shooting out from the seed, shot beneath,
   And a vast world of waters around him
   In furious torrents began.

4. Then he sunk, & around his spent Lungs
   Began intricate pipes that drew in
   The spawn of the waters. Outbranching
   An immense Fibrous form, stretching out
   Thro' the bottoms of immensity, raging,

5. He rose on the floods; then he smote
   The wild deep with his terrible wrath
   Seperating the heavy and thin.

6. Down the heavy sunk, cleaving around
   To the fragments of solid: up rose
   The thin, flowing round the fierce fires
   That glow'd furious in the expanse.

Chap: IV

1. Then Light first began: from the fires,
   Beams, conducted by fluid so pure,
   Flow'd around the Immense, Los beheld
   Forthwith writhing upon the dark void
   The Back bone of Urizen appear
   Hurtling upon the wind
   Like a serpent! like an iron chain
   Whirling about in the Deep.

2. Upfolding his Fibres together
   To a Form of impregnable strength,
   Los, astonish'd and terrified, built
   Furnaces; he formed an Anvil,
   A Hammer of adamant: then began
   The binding of Urizen day and night.

3. Circling round the dark Demon, with howlings
   Dismay & sharp blightings, the Prophet
   Of Eternity beat on his iron links.

4. And first, from those infinite fires,
   The light that flow'd down on the winds
   He siez'd, beating incessant, condensing
   The subtil particles in an Orb.

5. Roaring indignant the bright sparks
   Endur'd the vast Hammer; but unwearied
   Los beat on the Anvil, till glorious
   An immense Orb of fire he fram'd.

6. Oft he quench'd it beneath in the Deeps;
   Then survey'd the all bright mass. Again
   Siezing fires from the terrific Orbs,
   He heated the round Globe; then beat,
   While roaring his furnaces endur'd
   The chain'd Orb in their infinite wombs.

7. Nine ages completed their circles
   When Los heated the glowing mass, casting
   It down into the Deeps: the Deeps fled
   Away in redounding smoke: the Sun
   Stood self-balanc'd. And Los smil'd with joy.
   He the vast Spine of Urizen siez'd
   And bound down to the glowing illusion.

8. But no light; for the Deep fled away
   On all sides, and left an unform'd
   Dark vacuity: here Urizen lay
   In fierce torments on his glowing bed,

9. Till his Brain in a rock, & his Heart
   In a fleshy slough formed four rivers
   Obscuring the immense Orb of fire
   Flowing down into night; till a Form
   Was completed, a Human Illusion
   In darkness and deep clouds involv'd.

                The End of the
                Book of LOS

THE BOOK OF AHANIA

(1795)

Chap: 1st

1. Fuzon on a chariot iron-wing'd
   On spiked flames rose: his hot visage
   Flam'd furious; sparkles his hair & beard
   Shot down his wide bosom and shoulders.
   On clouds of smoke rages his chariot,
   And his right hand burns red in its cloud,
   Moulding into a vast globe his wrath
   As the thunder-stone is moulded,
   Son of Urizen's silent burnings.

2. 'Shall we worship this Demon of smoke,'
   Said Fuzon, 'this abstract non-entity,
   This cloudy God seated on waters,
   Now seen, now obscur'd, King of Sorrow?'

3. So he spoke in a fiery flame,
   On Urizen frowning indignant,
   The Globe of wrath shaking on high.
   Roaring with fury, he threw
   The howling Globe; burning it flew,
   Length'ning into a hungry beam. Swiftly

4. Oppos'd to the exulting flam'd beam
   The broad Disk of Urizen upheav'd
   Across the Void many a mile.

5. It was forg'd in mills where the winter
   Beats incessant: ten winters the disk
   Unremitting endur'd the cold hammer.

6. But the strong arm that sent it remember'd
   The sounding beam: laughing, it tore through
   That beaten mass, keeping its direction,
   The cold loins of Urizen dividing.

7. Dire shriek'd his invisible Lust.
   Deep groan'd Urizen! stretching his awful hand,
   Ahania (so name his parted soul)
   He siez'd on his mountains of Jealousy.
   He groan'd, anguish'd, & called her Sin,
   Kissing her and weeping over her;
   Then hid her in darkness, in silence,
   Jealous tho' she was invisible.

8. She fell down, a faint shadow wand'ring
   In chaos and circling dark Urizen
   As the moon, anguish'd, circles the earth:
   Hopeless! abhorr'd! a death-shadow
   Unseen, unbodied, unknown,
   The mother of Pestilence.

9. But the fiery beam of Fuzon
   Was a pillar of fire to Egypt
   Five hundred years wand'ring on earth
   Till Los siez'd it and beat in a mass
   With the body of the sun.

Chap: II^d

1. But the forehead of Urizen gathering,
   And his eyes pale with anguish, his lips
   Blue & changing, in tears and bitter
   Contrition, he prepar'd his Bow

2. Form'd of Ribs that in his dark solitude,
   When obscur'd in his forests, fell monsters
   Arose. For his dire Contemplations
   Rush'd down like floods from his mountains,
   In torrents of mud settling thick
   With Eggs of unnatural production:
   Forthwith hatching, some howl'd on his hills,
   Some in vales, some aloft flew in air.

3. Of these, an enormous dread Serpent,
   Scaled and poisonous horned,
   Approach'd Urizen even to his knees
   As he sat on his dark rooted Oak.

4. With his horns he push'd furious:
   Great the conflict & great the jealousy
   In cold poisons: but Urizen smote him.

5. First he poison'd the rocks with his blood,
   Then polish'd his ribs, and his sinews
   Dried, laid them apart till winter;
   Then a Bow black prepar'd; on this Bow
   A poisoned rock plac'd in silence.
   He utter'd these words to the Bow:

6. 'O Bow of the clouds of secrecy,
   O nerve of that lust form'd monster!
   Send this rock swift invisible thro'
   The black clouds on the bosom of Fuzon.'

7. So saying, In torment of his wounds,
   He bent the enormous ribs slowly:
   A circle of darkness! then fixed
   The sinew in its rest; then the Rock,
   Poisonous source! plac'd with art, lifting difficult
   Its weighty bulk: silent the rock lay,

8. While Fuzon, his tygers unloosing,
   Thought Urizen slain by his wrath.
   'I am God,' said he, 'eldest of things!'

9. Sudden sings the rock: swift & invisible
   On Fuzon flew: enter'd his bosom.
   His beautiful visage, his tresses
   That gave light to the mornings of heaven,
   Were smitten with darkness, deform'd
   And outstretch'd on the edge of the forest.

10. But the rock fell upon the Earth,
    Mount Sinai in Arabia.

Chap: III

1. The Globe shook, and Urizen, seated
   On black clouds, his sore wound anointed;
   The ointment flow'd down on the void
   Mix'd with blood: here the snake gets her poison.

2. With difficulty & great pain Urizen
   Lifted on high the dead corse:
   On his shoulders he bore it to where
   A Tree hung over the Immensity.

3. For when Urizen shrunk away
   From Eternals, he sat on a rock

Barren: a rock which himself
From redounding fancies had petrified.
Many tears fell on the rock,
Many sparks of vegetation.
Soon shot the pained root
Of Mystery under his heel.
It grew a thick tree: he wrote
In silence his book of iron,
Till the horrid plant, bending its boughs,
Grew to roots when it felt the earth
And again sprung to many a tree.

4. Amaz'd started Urizen! when
   He beheld himself compassed round
   And high roofed over with trees.
   He arose, but the stems stood so thick
   He with difficulty and great pain
   Brought his Books, all but the Book
   Of iron, from the dismal shade.

5. The Tree still grows over the Void,
   Enrooting itself all around,
   And endless labyrinth of woe!

6. The corse of his first begotten
   On the accursed Tree of Mystery,
   On the topmost stem of this Tree
   Urizen nail'd Fuzon's corse.

Chap: IV

1. Forth flew the arrows of pestilence
   Round the pale living Corse on the tree;

2. For in Urizen's slumbers of abstraction
   In the infinite ages of Eternity,
   When his Nerves of Joy melted and flow'd
   A white Lake on the dark blue air,
   In perturb'd pain and dismal torment
   Now stretching out, now swift conglobing,

3. Effluvia vapour'd above
   In noxious clouds; these hover'd thick
   Over the disorganiz'd Immortal,
   Till petrific pain scurf'd o'er the Lakes
   As the bones of man, solid & dark,

4. The clouds of disease hover'd wide
   Around the Immortal in torment,
   Perching around the hurtling bones,
   Disease on disease, shape on shape,
   Winged, screaming in blood & torment.

5. The Eternal Prophet beat on his anvils,
   Enrag'd in the desolate darkness,
   He forg'd nets of iron around
   And Los threw them around the bones.

6. The shapes screaming flutter'd vain:
   Some combin'd into muscles & glands,
   Some organs for craving and lust;
   Most remain'd on the tormented void,
   Urizen's army of horrors.

7. Round the pale living Corse on the Tree
   Forty years flew the arrows of pestilence.

8. Wailing and terror and woe
   Ran thro' all his dismal world
   Forty years; all his sons & daughters
   Felt their skulls harden; then Asia
   Arose in the pendulous deep.

9. They reptilize upon the Earth.

10. Fuzon groan'd on the Tree.

Chap: V

1. The lamenting voice of Ahania
   Weeping upon the void
   And round the Tree of Fuzon:
   Distant in solitary night
   Her voice was heard, but no form
   Had she; but her tears from clouds
   Eternal fell round the Tree.

2. And the voice cried: 'Ah, Urizen! Love!
   Flower of morning! I weep on the verge
   Of Non-entity: how wide the Abyss
   Between Ahania and thee!

3. 'I lie on the verge of the deep,
   I see thy dark clouds ascend,
   I see thy black forests and floods
   A horrible waste to my eyes!

4. 'Weeping I walk over rocks,
   Over dens & thro' valleys of death.
   Why didst thou despise Ahania,
   To cast me from thy bright presence
   Into the World of Loneness?

5. 'I cannot touch his hand,
   Nor weep on his knees, nor hear
   His voice & bow, nor see his eyes
   And joy, nor hear his footsteps and
   My heart leap at the lovely sound!
   I cannot kiss the place
   Whereon his bright feet have trod,
   But I wander on the rocks
   With hard necessity.

6. 'Where is my golden palace?
   Where my ivory bed?
   Where the joy of my morning hour?
   Where the sons of eternity singing

7. 'To awake bright Urizen, my king,
   To arise to the mountain sport,
   To the bliss of eternal valleys:

8. 'To awake my king in the morn
   To embrace Ahania's joy
   On the bredth of his open bosom,
   From my soft cloud of dew to fall
   In showers of life on his harvests?

9. 'When he gave my happy soul
   To the sons of eternal joy:
   When he took the daughters of life
   Into my chambers of love:

10. 'When I found babes of bliss on my beds,
    And bosoms of milk in my chambers
    Fill'd with eternal seed,
    O! eternal births sung round Ahania
    In interchange sweet of their joys.

11. 'Swell'd with ripeness & fat with fatness,
    Bursting on winds my odors,
    My ripe figs and rich pomegranates
    In infant joy at thy feet
    O Urizen, sported and sang.

12. 'Then thou with thy lap full of seed,
    With thy hand full of generous fire,
    Walked forth from the clouds of morning,
    On the virgins of springing joy,
    On the human soul to cast
    The seed of eternal science.

13. 'The sweat poured down thy temples
    To Ahania return'd in evening;
    The moisture awoke to birth
    My mother's-joys, sleeping in bliss.

14. 'But now, alone, over rocks, mountains,
    Cast out from thy lovely bosom,
    Cruel jealousy, selfish fear,
    Self-destroying: how can delight
    Renew in these chains of darkness
    Where bones of beasts are strown
    On the bleak and snowy mountains
    Where bones from the birth are buried
    Before they see the light?'

FINIS

From VALA

Night the Ninth

Luvah & Vala woke, & all the sons & daughters of
    Luvah
Awoke; they wept to one another & they reascended
To the Eternal Man in woe: he cast them wailing into
The world of shadows, thro' the air, till winter is over
    & gone;
But the Human Wine stood wondering; in all their
    delightful Expanses
The elements subside; the heavens roll'd on with vocal
    harmony.

Then Los, who is Urthona, rose in all his regenerate
    power.
The Sea that roll'd & foam'd with darkness & the
    shadows of death
Vomited out & gave up all; the floods lift up their
    hands
Singing & shouting to the Man; they bow their hoary
    heads
And murmuring in their channels flow & circle round
    his feet.

Then Dark Urthona took the Corn out of the Stores of
    Urizen;
He ground it in his rumbling Mills. Terrible the
    distress

Of all the Nations of Earth, ground in the Mills of
    Urthona.
In his hand Tharmas takes the Storms: he turns the
    whirlwind loose
Upon the wheels; the stormy seas howl at his dread
    command
And Eddying fierce rejoice in the fierce agitation of the
    wheels
Of Dark Urthona. Thunders, Earthquakes, Fires,
    Water floods,
Rejoice to one another; loud their voices shake the
    Abyss,
Their dread forms tending the dire mills. The grey
    hoar frost was there,
And his pale wife, the aged Snow; they watch over the
    fires,
They build the Ovens of Urthona. Nature in darkness
    groans
And Men are bound to sullen contemplation in the
    night:
Restless they turn on beds of sorrow; in their inmost
    brain
Feeling the crushing Wheels, they rise, they write the
    bitter words
Of Stern Philosophy & knead the bread of knowledge
    with tears & groans.

Such are the works of Dark Urthona. Tharmas sifted
    the corn.
Urthona made the Bread of Ages, & he placed it,
In golden & in silver baskets, in heavens of precious
    stone
And then took his repose in Winter, in the night of
    Time.

The Sun has left his blackness & has found a fresher
    morning,
And the mild moon rejoices in the clear & cloudless
    night,
And Man walks forth from midst of the fires: the evil is
    all consum'd.
His eyes behold the Angelic spheres arising night &
    day;
The stars consum'd like a lamp blown out, & in their
    stead, behold
The Expanding Eyes of Man behold the depths of
    wondrous worlds!
One Earth, one sea beneath; nor Erring Globes
    wander, but Stars
Of fire rise up nightly from the Ocean; & one Sun
Each morning, like a New born Man, issues with songs
    & joy
Calling the Plowman to his Labour & the Shepherd to
    his rest.

He walks upon the Eternal Mountains, raising his
     heavenly voice,
Conversing with the Animal forms of wisdom night &
     day,
That, risen from the Sea of fire, renew'd walk o'er the
     Earth;
For Tharmas brought his flocks upon the hills, & in the
     Vales
Around the Eternal Man's bright tent, the little
     Children play
Among the wooly flocks. The hammer of Urthona
     sounds
In the deep caves beneath; his limbs renew'd, his Lions
     roar
Around the Furnaces & in Evening sport upon the
     plains.
They raise their faces from the Earth, conversing with
     the Man:

'How is it we have walk'd thro' fires & yet are not
     consum'd?
'How is it that all things are chang'd, even as in ancient
     times?'

The Sun arises from his dewy bed, & the fresh airs
Play in his smiling beams giving the seeds of life to
     grow,

And the fresh Earth beams forth ten thousand
    thousand springs of life.
Urthona is arisen in his strength, no longer now
Divided from Enitharmon, no longer the Spectre Los.
Where is the Spectre of Prophecy? where the delusive
    Phantom?
Departed: & Urthona rises from the ruinous Walls
In all his ancient strength to form the golden armour
    of science
For intellectual War. The war of swords departed now,
The dark Religions are departed & sweet Science
    reigns.

End of The Dream

ANNOTATIONS TO SWEDENBORG'S WISDOM OF ANGELS CONCERNING DIVINE LOVE AND DIVINE WISDOM

London MDCCLXXXVIII
Written about 1789

There can be no Good Will. Will is always Evil; it is persecution to others or selfishness. If God is anything he is Understanding. He is the Influx from that into the Will. Good to others or benevolent Understanding comes [?] to Will continually, but never comes ..., because Man is only Evil ...

Understanding or Thought is not natural to Man; it is acquir'd by means of Suffering & Distress i.e. Experience. Will, Desire, Love, Pain, Envy, & all other affections are Natural, but Understanding is Acquired ...

[The remainder of this passage, which is written in pencil on the flyleaf, is illegible. The subsequent annotations are marginal, and are here printed after the corresponding passages from Swedenborg's text, these being given in smaller type. Words underlined by Blake are printed in italic.]

Doth it not happen that in Proportion as the Affection which is of Love groweth cold, the Thought, Speech and Action grow cold also? And that in Proportion as it is heated, they also are heated? But this a wise Man perceiveth, not from a Knowledge that Love is the Life of Man, but from Experience of this Fact.

They also percieve this from Knowledge, but not with the natural part.

No one knowth what is the Life of Man, unless he knoweth that it is Love.

This was known to me & thousands.

That the Divine or God is not in Space ... cannot be comprehended by any merely natural Idea, but it may by a spiritual Idea: The Reason why it cannot be comprehended by a natural Idea is because in that Idea there is Space.

What a natural Idea is.

Nevertheless, Man may comprehend this by natural Thought, if he will only admit into such Thought somewhat of spiritual Light.

Mark this.

A spiritual Idea doth not derive any Thing from Space, but it derives every Thing appertaining to it from State.

Poetic idea.

Pages 8–9.

Hence it may appear, that Man from a *merely natural* Idea cannot comprehend that the Divine is every where, and yet not in Space; and yet that Angels and Spirits clearly comprehend this; consequently *that Man also may*, if so be he will admit something of spiritual Light into his Thought; the Reason why Man may comprehend it is because his Body doth not think, but his Spirit, therefore not his natural but his spiritual Part.

Observe the distinction here between Natural & Spiritual as seen by Man. Man may comprehend, but not the natural or external man.

Page 10.

It hath been said, that in the spiritual World Spaces appear equally as in the natural World. ... Hence it is that the Lord, although he is in the Heavens with the Angels everywhere, nevertheless appears high above them as a Sun: And whereas the reception of Love and Wisdom constitutes Affinity with him, therefore those Heavens appear nearer to him where the Angels are in a nearer Affinity from Reception, than where they are in a more remote Affinity.

He who Loves feels love descend into him & if he has wisdom may percieve it is from the Poetic Genius, which is the Lord.

Page 11.

In all the Heavens there is no other Idea of God than that of a Man.

Man can have no idea of any thing greater than Man, as a cup cannot contain more than its capaciousness. But God is a man, not because he is so perciev'd by man, but because he is the creator of man.

'The Gentiles, particularly the Africans ... entertain an Idea of God as of a Man, and say that no one can have any other Idea of God: When they hear that many form an Idea of God as existing in the Midst of a Cloud, they ask where such are....'

Think of a white cloud as being holy, you cannot love it; but think of a holy man within the cloud, love springs up in your thoughts, for to think of holiness distinct from man is impossible to the affections. Thought alone can make monsters, but the affections cannot.

They who are wiser than the common People pronounce God to be invisible.

Worldly wisdom, or demonstration by the senses is the cause of this.

The Negation of God constitutes Hell, and in the Christian World the Negation of the Lord's Divinity.

The Negation of the Poetic Genius.

When Love is in Wisdom, then it existeth. These two are such a ONE, that they may be distinguished indeed in Thought, but not in Act.

Thought without affection makes a distinction between Love & Wisdom, as it does between body & Spirit.

267

What Person of Sound Reason doth not perceive, that the Divine is not divisible ... If another, who hath no Reason, should say that it is possible there may be several Infinities, Uncreates, Omnipotents and Gods, provided they have the same Essence, and that thereby there is one Infinite, Uncreate, Omnipotent and God – is not one and the same Essence one and the same Identity?

Answer: Essence is not Identity, but from Essence proceeds Identity & from one Essence may proceed many Identities, as from one Affection may proceed many thoughts. Surely this is an oversight.

That there is but one Omnipotent, Uncreate & God I agree, but that there is but one Infinite I do not; for if all but God is not Infinite, they shall come to an End, which God forbid.

If the Essence was the same as the Identity, there could be but one Identity, which is false. Heaven would upon this plan be but a Clock; but one & the same Essence is therefore Essence & not Identity.

Appearances are the first Things from which the human Mind forms its Understanding, and it cannot shake them off but by an Investigation of the Cause, and if the Cause is very deep, it cannot investigate it, *without keeping the Understanding some Time in spiritual Light.* ...

This Man can do while in the body.

It cannot be demonstrated except by such Things as a Man can perceive by his bodily Senses.

Demonstration is only by bodily Senses.

Page 40.
With respect to God, it is not possible that he can love and be reciprocally beloved by others, in whom ... there is any Thing Divine; for if there was any Thing Divine in them, then it would not be beloved by others, but it would love itself.

False. Take it so or the contrary, it comes to the same, for if a thing loves it is infinite. Perhaps we only differ in the meaning of the words Infinity & Eternal.

Page 56.
Man is only a Recipient of Life. From this Cause it is, that Man, from his own hereditary Evil, reacts against God; but so far as he believes that all his Life is from God, and every Good of Life from the Action of God, and every Evil of Life from the Reaction of Man, Reaction thus becomes correspondent with Action, and Man acts with God as from himself.

Good & Evil are here both Good & the two contraries Married.

Page 57.
But he who knows how to elevate his Mind above the Ideas of Thought which are derived from Space and Time, such a Man passes from Darkness to Light, and becomes wise in Things spiritual and Divine ... and then by Virtue of that Light he shakes off the Darkness of natural Light, and removes *its Fallacies* from the Center to the Circumference.

When the fallacies of darkness are in the circumference they cast a bound about the infinite.

269

Page 58.
Now inasmuch as the Thoughts of the Angels derive nothing from Space and Time, but from States of Life, it is evident that they do not comprehend what is meant when it is said, that the Divine fills Space, for they do not know what Space is, but that they comprehend clearly, when it is said, without any Idea of Space that the Divine fills all Things.

Excellent.

Page 131.
That without two Suns, the one living and the other dead, there can be no Creation.

False philosophy according to the letter, but true according to the spirit.

Page 133.
It follows that the one Sun is living and that the other Sun is dead, also that the dead Sun itself was created by the living Sun from the Lord.

How could Life create death?

The reason why a dead Sun was created is to the End that in the Ultimate all Things may be fixed. .... On this and no other Ground Creation is founded. The terraqueous Globe ... is as it were the Basis and Firmament.

They exist literally about the sun & not about the earth.

That all Things were created from the Lord by the living Sun, *and nothing by the dead Sun*, may appear from this Consideration. ....

The dead Sun is only a phantasy of evil Man.

Page 146.
It is the same upon Earth with Men, but with this Difference, that the Angels feel that Heat and see that Light, whereas Men do not....

He speaks of Men as meer earthly Men, not as receptacles of spirit, or else he contradicts N. 257 [p. 220].

Now forasmuch as Man, whilst he is in natural Heat and Light, knoweth nothing of spiritual Heat and Light in himself, and this cannot be known but by Experience from the spiritual World....

This is certainly not to be understood according to the letter, for it is false by all experience. Who does not or may not know of love & wisdom in himself?

Page 181.
From these Considerations a Conclusion was drawn, that the Whole of Charity and Faith is in Works....

The Whole of the New Church is in the Active Life & not in Ceremonies at all.

Pages 195–6.
These three Degrees of Altitude are named Natural, Spiritual and Celestial. ... Man, at his Birth, first comes into the natural Degree, and this increases in him by Continuity according to the Sciences, and according to the Understanding acquired by them, to the Summit of Understanding which is called Rational.

Study Sciences till you are blind, Study intellectuals till you are cold, Yet science cannot teach intellect. Much less can intellect teach Affection. How foolish then is it to assert that Man is born in only one degree, when that one degree is reception of the 3 degrees, two of which he must destroy or close up or they will descend; if he closes up the two superior, then he is not truly in the 3ᵈ, but descends out of it into meer Nature or Hell. See N. 239 [p. 198]. Is it not also evident that one degree will not open the other, & that science will not open intellect, but that they are discrete & not continuous so as to explain each other except by correspondence, which has nothing to do with demonstration; for you cannot demonstrate one degree by the other; for how can science be brought to demonstrate intellect without making them continuous & not discrete?

Page 196.
Man, so long as he lives in the World, does not know any Thing of the opening of these Degrees in himself.

See N. 239 [p. 198].

Page 198.
In every Man there is a natural, spiritual and celestial Will and Understanding, in Power from his Birth, and in Act whilst they are opening.

Mark this; it explains no. 238 [p. 196].

In a Word the Mind of Man ... is of three Degrees, so that ... a Man may be elevated thereby to Angelic Wisdom and possess it, while he lives in the World, but nevertheless he does not come into it till after Death, if he becomes an Angel *and then he speaks Things ineffable and incomprehensible to the natural Man.*

Not to a Man, but to the natural Man.

Page 200.
Every one who consults his Reason, *whilst it is in the Light,* may see that Man's Love is the End of all Things appertaining to him.

Page 204.
And hence it also follows that the Understanding does not lead the Will, or that Wisdom does not produce Love, but that it only teaches and shows the Way, it teaches how a Man ought to live, and shows the Way in which he ought to walk.

Mark this.

Page 219.
From this it is evident, that Man, *so long as he lives in the World, and is thereby in the natural Degree,* cannot be elevated into Wisdom itself, ...

See Sect. 4 of the next Number.

Page 220.
But still Man, in whom the spiritual Degree is open, comes into that Wisdom when he dies, and may also come into it by laying asleep the Sensations of the Body, and by Influx from above at the Same time into the Spirituals of his Mind.

This is while in the Body.

This is to be understood as unusual in our time, but common in ancient.

The natural Mind of Man consists of spiritual Substances, and at the same Time of natural Substances; from its *spiritual Substances* Thought is produced, but not from its *natural Substances*; ...

Many perversely understand him as if man, while in the body, was only conversant with natural Substances, because themselves are mercenary & worldly & have no idea of any but worldly gain.

Page 233.
... for the natural Man can elevate his Understanding to superior Light as far as he desires it, but he who is principled in Evils and thence in Things false, does not elevate it higher than to the superior Region of his natural Mind; ...

273

Who shall dare to say after this that all elevation is of self & is Enthusiasm & Madness, & is it not plain that self-derived intelligence is worldly demonstration?

Page 268.
Forasmuch as the Things, which constitute the Sun of the spiritual World, are from the Lord, and not the Lord, therefore they are not Life in itself, ...

This assertion that the spiritual Sun is not Life explains how the natural Sun is dead.

This is an Arcanum which the Angels by their spiritual Ideas can see in Thought, and also express in Speech, but not Men by their *natural Ideas*; ...

How absurd then would it be to say that no man on earth has a spiritual idea after reading N. 257 [p. 220].

Page 269.
That there is such a Difference between the Thoughts of Angels and Men, was made known to me by this Experience. They were told to think of something spiritually, and afterwards to tell me what they thought of; when this was done and would have told me, they could not, ...

They could not tell him in natural ideas; how absurd must men be to understand him as if he said the angels could not express themselves at all to him.

Page 276.
Forasmuch as there is such a Progression of the Fibres and Vessels in a Man from first Principles to Ultimates, therefore there is a similar Progression of their States; their States are the Sensations, Thoughts and Affections; these also from their first Principles *where they are in the Light*, pervade to their Ultimates, where they are in Obscurity; or from their first Principles, where they are in Heat, to their Ultimates where they are not *in Heat.*

274

We see here that the cause of an ultimate is the absence from heat & light.

Page 285.
It is to be observed, that the Heat, Light and Atmospheres of the natural World conduce nothing to this Image of Creation, ...

Therefore the Natural Earth & Atmosphere is a Phantasy.

The Heat, Light and Atmospheres of the natural World only open Seeds; ... but this not by Powers derived from their own Sun ...

Mark this.

Page 286.
... but by Powers from the spiritual Sun, ... *for the Image of Creation is Spiritual,* nevertheless that it may appear, and furnish Use *in the natural World,* ... it must be clothed in Matter ...

... it is evident, that as there is a Resemblance of Creation in the Forms of Vegetables, so there is also in the Forms of Animals, viz. that there is a Progression from first Principles to Ultimates, and from Ultimates to first Principles.

A going forth & returning.

Page 295.
... there doth not exist any Thing in the created Universe, which hath not Correspondence with Something of Man, not only with his Affections and his Thoughts thence derived, but also with the Organs and Viscera of his Body, not with them as Substances, but with them as Uses.

Uses & substances are so different as not to correspond.

Pages 410–411.
Thought indeed exists first, because it is of the natural Mind, but Thought from the Perception of Truth, *which is from the Affection of Truth, exists last; this Thought is the Thought of Wisdom, but the other is Thought from the Memory by the Sight of the natural Mind.*

Note this.

Page 421.
From these Things it may be seen, that Love or the Will joins itself to Wisdom or the Understanding, and not that Wisdom or the Understanding joins itself to Love or the Will.

Mark this.

Page 422.
Thoughts, Perceptions, and Knowledge, thence derived, flow indeed from the spiritual World, *but still they are not received by the Understanding, but by the Love according to its Affections in the Understanding.*

Mark this.

It appears also as if the Understanding joined itself to Love or the Will, *but this also is a Fallacy;* Love or the Will joins itself to the Understanding and causeth the Understanding to be reciprocally joined to it.

Mark this.

Page 423.
For the life of Man is his Love, ... that is, according as he has exalted his Affections by Truths, ...

Mark this.

Page 424.
From these Considerations it is also evident, *that Love joins itself to the Understanding, and not vice versa. ...*

Mark this.

Page 425.

He who knows all the Fabric of the Lungs from Anatomy, if he compares them with the Understanding, may clearly see that the *Understanding does nothing from itself,* that it does not *perceive nor think from itself, but all from Affections which are of the Love,* which in the Understanding are called the Affection of knowing, ...

Mark.

Page 426.

From the Structure of the Lungs ... *I was fully convinced that the Love by its Affections joins itself to the Understanding, and that the Understanding does not join itself to any Affection of the Love.* ...

Mark this.

Pages 426–427.

That Wisdom or the Understanding by Means of the Power given it by Love, can be elevated, and receive the Things which are of the Light from Heaven, and perceive them.

Mark this.

Page 429.

... when Man shuns Evils as Sins, therefore by these Means Love or the Will also can be elevated, and without these Means it cannot.

Is it not false then, that love recieves influx thro' the understanding, as was asserted in the society?

Page 435.

... and moreover this Love became impure by Reason of the Separation of celestial Love from it in the Parents.

Therefore it was not created impure & is not naturally so.

277

Page 436.
... so far the Love is purged of its Uncleannesses, and purified, that is, so far it is elevated into the Heat of Heaven, ... in which the Understanding is.

Therefore it does not recieve influx thro' the understanding.

Page 440.
That Love or the Will is defiled in the Understanding, and by it, if they are not elevated together.

Mark this: they are elevated together.

Page 441.
The Understanding is not made spiritual and celestial, but the Love is;...

Page 458.
Moreover it was shown in the Light of Heaven, ... that the interior Compages of this little Brain was ... in the Order and Form of Heaven; and that its exterior Compages was in Opposition to that Order and Form.

Heaven & Hell are born together.

278

INDEX OF FIRST LINES